# FOG AND LIGHT

## San Francisco through the Eyes of the Poets Who Live Here

### Selected by Diane Frank

BLUE LIGHT PRESS ◆ 1ST WORLD PUBLISHING

SAN FRANCISCO ◆ FAIRFIELD ◆ DELHI

*Fog and Light:*
*San Francisco through the Eyes of the Poets Who Live Here*

"Dog" by Lawrence Ferlinghetti, from *A Coney Island of the Mind*, © 1958 by Lawrence Ferlinghetti. Reprinted by permission of New Directions Publishing Corporation.

BLUE LIGHT PRESS
www.bluelightpress.com
Email: bluelightpress@aol.com

Poems selected by Diane Frank
Chief Editor, Blue Light Press

Book & Cover Design: Melanie Gendron

Cover Photographs: Jeffrey S. Bartfeld
Front Image: "Rainy Afternoon at the Golden Gate"
Back Image: "San Francisco Dawn from Sausalito"

Library of Congress Cataloging-in-Publication Data

ISBN: 978-1-4218-3689-8

# Fog and Light

San Francisco through the Eyes
of the Poets Who Live Here

# Contents

# Welcome to San Francisco!

When I see a group of tourists at Fisherman's Wharf or Union Square, I can't help thinking that this is not the San Francisco where the rest of us live. Yes, I love riding cable cars as much as any tourist and enjoy a bowl of clam chowder at Boudin's, but there's a better San Francisco and a deeper San Francisco than most tourists know.

In this book of poems written by San Francisco poets, we show you the city that most tourists miss — dancing the samba at Carnaval in the Mission District, getting up before dawn to photograph the Golden Gate Bridge with the perfect angle of light, the timpani of Pacific waves in the Outer Sunset, enjoying a cappuccino before work on Minna Alley, growing up on Liberty Street in Eureka Heights, browsing through Bird & Beckett Bookstore in Glen Park, the dog path at Fort Funston, walking home through the Civic Center in Sunday heat, the clatter inside a flat on Nob Hill next to the cable car tracks, ushering on opening night at the San Francisco Opera, an inside view of the Haight Ashbury during the Summer of Love, rush hour at the Montgomery Street BART Station, the Sing It Yourself Messiah with the Golden Gate Symphony, a group of eight-year-old friends in Bayview careening down their street on a board attached to a roller skate, riding to school on the 6 Masonic bus, the Doggie Diner, a night game at Candlestick Park, the Alemany Farmer's Market, the lively street scene at 16th and Valencia, riding the N Judah street car with two cellos to play Mahler at the Herbst Theatre on Bay to Breakers Sunday — and so much more.

As the editor of this book, I feel like the curator of a gallery of fine art. The art is our City. Welcome and enjoy!

Blessings,
Diane Frank, Chief Editor
Blue Light Press

# Dog

The dog trots freely in the street
and sees reality
and the things he sees
are bigger than himself
and the things he sees
are his reality
Drunks in doorways
Moons on trees
The dog trots freely thru the street
and the things he sees
are smaller than himself
Fish on newsprint
Ants in holes
Chickens in Chinatown windows
their heads a block away
The dog trots freely in the street
and the things he smells
smell something like himself
The dog trots freely in the street
past puddles and babies
cats and cigars
poolrooms and policemen
He doesn't hate cops
He merely has no use for them
and he goes past them
and past the dead cows hung up whole
in front of the San Francisco Meat Market
He would rather eat a tender cow
than a tough policeman
though either might do
And he goes past the Romeo Ravioli Factory
and past Coit's Tower

and past Congressman Doyle
He's afraid of Coit's Tower
but he's not afraid of Congressman Doyle
although what he hears is very discouraging
very depressing
very absurd
to a sad young dog like himself
to a serious dog like himself
But he has his own free world to live in
His own fleas to eat
He will not be muzzled
Congressman Doyle is just another
fire hydrant
to him
The dog trots freely in the street
and has his own dog's life to live
and to think about
and to reflect upon
touching and tasting and testing everything
investigating everything
without benefit of perjury
a real realist
with a real tale to tell
and a real tail to tell it with
a real live
      barking
           democratic dog
engaged in real
           free enterprise
with something to say
           about ontology
something to say
           about reality
               and how to see it
                   and how to hear it

with his head cocked sideways
                              at streetcorners
as if he is just about to have
                              his picture taken
                                        for Victor Records
                    listening for
                              His Master's Voice
          and looking
                    like a living questionmark
                              into the
                              great gramaphone
                              of puzzling existence
with its wondrous hollow horn
          which always seems
          just about to spout forth
                              some Victorious answer
                              to everything

## The Call of the West

*"We are homesick most for the places we have never known."*
*– Carson McCullers*

White fingers of fog grasp the bridge
as if to lift it from its moorings
along the headlands of Marin and San Francisco —

the strait named Golden Gate, once home of the Ohlone,
place where white, shark-fin sails
slice the water's blues and grays, and in the distance,
a miles-long, hump-backed whale of thick mist
rolls over hills beneath which humans teem like krill.

In salty air fog horns keen outside walls
where poets lift their voices over beer
sitting next to gas log fireplaces,
and sweethearts hear symphonies
after fragrant, wine-splashed meals,
where cold winds of street canyons carry sounds
of homeless pleading for coins and kindness
between raw coughs and schizophrenic outbursts,
as they stand in line for meals at Glide and St. Anthony's;
where Monterey cypresses green a golden park,
where bullets suddenly rip the air, where gays have married.

Up close, where fog chills or sunbeams heat its soft winds,
this people-plashed cove at the edge of creation
holds all colors, all stripes, all ages, all tongues
in its tender St. Francis embrace, its unconditional hippie hug.

# Kaliflower Commune

On Clayton Street at Oak,
six of us shared a house
and a cat named Martha My Dear.
The Haight-Ashbury Free Clinic
was our next block neighbor.
We ate together, lit menorahs,
decorated Christmas trees,
and packed for Redwood forest
camping trips above the Russian River,
stopping to visit
deeded-to-God Morning Star Ranch
as we drove back home.
I still see Eddie's smile-wide face
rushing into our Victorian's foyer
holding up the released-that-day
Joni Mitchell *Blue* album.

Two years later, inside a three-story
building on Arguello Street,
I lived with lesbians in a middle flat,
egg salad between
top and bottom floors
of gay boy rye bread.

The Mime Troupe/Diggers
lit the Haight on fire in '67.
Their first Human Be-In in January
flamed into The Summer of Love,
then roared as a coffin-burning funeral pyre —
*The Death of the Hippie,* by October.
The wizards of this Oz
were signaling everyone to go back home by then.
Forget San Francisco and flowers in your hair,

Sgt. Pepper, and the Dead —
stay in Muskogee and Cincinnati.
The city was drowning in lost souls.

When I arrived in '69, I did not leave.
I knew something was happening —
an upbeat social earthquake
that made it safe to hitchhike …
and there were tight and fly-by-night
families of us living together everywhere.

Concentric ripples of the Digger sea change
lapped at our doors, touched us each week,
as a delivery of organic vegetables —
like a sacrament, and absolutely free.
And tucked inside the food box,
a wafer of graceful calligraphy
laced with psychedelic spirit art.
Kaliflower Commune ministered to
three hundred households of us.

By the early seventies, just before the drug war began,
the Digger/Free spirit of '67 still reached down into us
straight from 1640s England, from a rag tag group of poor
who had few tools back then to right the inequities of their time.
These Diggers fought with farming skills,
growing food on The Commons to share freely with all.

Most of us knew nothing about any of that
in our communal rooming houses,
but something in the air helped us trust
and have psychic wall-busting fun with one another.
This shiny, new, electric kool-aid tribal world
made us feel we had sprouted
hope-feathered wings that kept us hovering just above
all the things that wanted to bring us down.

Let thousands of fingers snap
in deafening beatnik ovation —
for Kaliflower, those ripped-jean angels.
They served us stories and veggie communion,
drew a vision-rich circle around
our Sancho Panza remnants.

# Postcard from the Castro

> *"Two days after I was elected I got a phone call and the voice was quite*
> *young. It was from Altoona, Pennsylvania. And the person said 'Thanks.'…*
> *If a bullet should enter my brain, let that bullet destroy every closet door.…*
> *You've gotta' give them hope."*
> *– Harvey Milk*

Harvey Milk is smiling out a window in the Castro again,
in a new portrait on the side of his old building —
half-circle smile, head bowed,
looking out through a sliver of sun
onto the sidewalk of his old neighborhood.

He seems to know something we don't.
Or is his smile just the start of a happy laugh
remembering this gay Mecca is named Eureka Valley?
Maybe he's simply admiring the beautiful boys
holding hands with such nonchalance
as they sashay past him heading toward
*Does Your Mother Know* on 18th Street.
He has the radiance of someone who sees through hate,
from this window on a wall, rainbow flag across his chest,
rainbows fluttering from lamp posts at every corner.

The van Gogh golds and blues of the mural
hang like a lodestar above his once open-to-all refuge,
his Castro Camera store, his first openly gay supervisor's
campaign office, this hippie community center
where I once sat in his old dentist's chair installed
like a work of beat art in the middle of his shop floor.
I knew him when I did not know who I was.

Looking back on the long journey from then to now:
his holy, disarming comedy silenced
by a deadly-serious, fear–spawned loathing …

yet out of that sudden, bloody silence, a roar —
from Altoona, Pennsylvania, San Antonio, Des Moines.

I have come here on a pilgrimage from the Haight:
I'm alive, I'm in love, I'm in hope, I'm out.
His image shines like a moon over Castro Street again,
but I cannot meet the gaze of his hidden, earthcast eyes.

If I could, I would say:
*Thanks, Harvey.*
*Having a wonderful time.*
*Wish you were here.*

## Winter of Love

*Valentine's Day San Francisco 2004*

At the front entrance of City Hall, exultant couples
walk out through open glass doors, holding hands
and licenses that flutter in their grasp like flags.

A tiptoe rain mizzles red, gold,
pink, lavender rose petals
quilting the palatial stone steps;
multi-colored umbrellas wait outside like limos.

The crowd cheers loudly every few minutes all day long,
as pair after pair of women, pair after pair of men
walks out through the city's gray mist
into rainbow, rainbow, rainbow.

# Golden Gate

Time like a tide
storms through this strait;
its charging waves bully
a mischievous bay,
spit and spray splash
in long slow drips,
myth and memory
on a young man's breaker.

He can almost see
a three-masted galleon,
hear its wooden moans,
smell its dank musk,
bobbing to the rhythm of the sea,
as it blindly sails past the narrow opening
of the Golden Gate.

He recalls the tale of his great grandfather,
crammed aboard a Clipper,
a week of canoes and mules through Panama,
then a U.S. mail ship,
miner's pick thrust beneath a cracked leather belt.

We all have dreams,
some that miss the harbor's entrance,
some that cat paw across
its foamy surges.

His dream has brought him
to this hulking, hunchback bay,
to the flowing shush of its waves,

which thump the barrier rocks,
and puddle the bouldered shore.

He chooses to live only
by this bay —
trusting its swells and troughs,
trusting its salty welcome.

# Urban Astronomy

**1.**

> Someone
> on the bus
> explains
> to anyone
> listening
> that the
> random objects
> in the street
>
> a wedding
> invitation
> torn in half
>
> a slice
> of bread
>
> three blood red
> oranges
>
> a set
> of keys
>
> have no doubt
> fallen
> from a passing
> comet
>
> we all
> look up

**2.**

> Memory
> is a
> planet
>
> unseen by
> the human
> eye
>
> Always moving
> away
> from its point
> of origin

**3.**

> She demonstrated
> the birth
> of the universe
> by throwing
> my shoes
> against the wall
>
> and kissing me

**4.**

> The light
> from the
> constantly burning
> sun
> comes through
> the openings
> in the venetian
> blind
> in pieces

striking my
books
at an
angle

then slowly
fading
in the
earth's
rotation

this is
what
death
looks like

to someone far away

## The Pleine Air Toilette of Madame X

A black swan
surrounded by down,
she emerges from a cocoon of sleep.

Awakened by the hum and churn of cement trucks,
the swoosh of cranes,
red steel stretching to the sky,
she reaches up
to cup the first ray of sun.

Holding a compact mirror,
she paints her lashes
thicker than Katy Perry's,
stroking them,
as the mist rises off sidewalks
at Mission and First.

Office workers clip and zip past
without a glance
at her open air boudoir.

Today her nightcap is red,
matching the lipstick
she draws on cool, chapped lips.
She rarely glances out her private dome
while preparing for the day.

I pick up a cappuccino down Minna Alley,
pass her again,
this time on her cell phone,
maybe ordering breakfast or
barking Buys on Wall Street
from her street-front office.

Her cube wall is made of cardboard
that she folds each morning
like sheets,
piles in a neat stack
under the No Parking sign
before stuffing her bedding into carry-on luggage.

Every morning she awakens on cold cement
sprinkled with feathers, pizza boxes, a few cigarette butts.
*I wonder what she would do if she got the flu...*

Some days she feeds pigeons in front of Walgreens
or across the street against the barbed wire fenced lot
and Portico Pizza,
discussing Plato or dogs
with the bearded man inside a garbage bag bed.

Yesterday I got to work late, passed
a well-dressed woman with familiar luggage
sitting on a bench
near the glass doors to my office tower.
I looked at her, twice:
Did we take the same painting class at Berkeley
or share a flight from Taipei?

Madame X was waiting,
in blue hat,
couture suit,
painted lashes,
ready for someone
to take her
away.

The next morning,
her spot was empty,

but for a few pigeons
pecking at high rise dust.

I never saw her again.

# Fog in Kensington

No waterfall of fog
ever tumbles into the bay
from the East Bay hills and Tilden Park.

The fog comes from the sea,
climbs over the seven San Francisco hills,
through the Golden Gate in a soft white river,
flows onto El Cerrito, Kensington,
its fingers crawl upwards from the flatlands
to claw its way uphill,
wrapping lampposts, bungalows, backyard redwoods,
in a cool white shroud.

But a few mornings a year
the fog rises only as high as the Arlington,
while Albany below remains covered under heavy mist.
The dawn warms the summit
above a sea of clouds,
extends across the Western horizon.

I sip the sunrise,
Tibetan God Realm view;
instead of train whistle,
automobile roar,
all I hear is
the coo of a mourning dove,
a crow caw,
and the occasional click
of a circadian clock.

## Coffee Augury

I stand in line —
ten or eleven hand-dripped coffees,
cappuccinos, lattes
ahead of me.

I'm behind a blue jeans couple
from the Mission,
twentyish,
slim, hipsters,
he has a star tattoo under his right ear,
other tattoos are hidden today.

His unshaved face is soft.
She keeps touching him,
twirling around him like ivy,
then unwraps her arms
to push him forward,
one foot closer to java.
Their fingers entwine.
He kisses her forehead with a half-smile,
looking outside
at mist rising over Mint Plaza.

Tall, a little stiff,
he yields to her whispers.
Their lips touch five times
before ordering
drip coffees and brioche;
then disappear on stools against
the wall of windows.

Donovan sighs
*wear your love like heaven ...*

My turn at the register.

La Marzocco Espresso machine
hisses, gurgles,
coffee grinder infuses
Indonesia into the room.

Today Aaron signed my coffee with a heart,
the milk foam art
floats in the center of my cup,
perfect
like the full moon.

Sugar crystals sink slowly as I stir.
the heart becomes a face —
my daily oracle.

## Brunch in San Francisco

The mantis wasn't praying
in front of Blue Bottle coffee;
she'd just finished her meal —
not a sour cherry brioche
or extra thick toast and espresso.

She'd eaten her lover,
slowly,
for several hours,
after their wild fling in Jessie alley,
doorway to Kyoto iced coffee
and cappuccinos with hearts.

Despite her meal,
she was stick thin
like the tattooed hipsters
standing in line for warm waffles and strawberries.

I arrived after he was a pile of shells,
blown across Mint Plaza.

She stared at me,
didn't want to leave her spot,
held onto the bottom of the blue and white sign,
watching flip flops, Roman sandals, high heeled boots.

Afraid she would be crushed,
I carried her to a patch of cape rush reeds,
fifteen feet of Gondwanan green
in a sea of granite and cement.

A man sipping a latte
lingered nearby.
I noticed him tapping his Doc Martins on the pavement
*I used to like Praying Mantises ...*

# Liberty Street

I've walked Tennessee Valley three times since it opened up last Monday. The trail has grown so lush and green during its Covid hiatus — nothing trampled. Bunnies scurry across the path. The trail ends at a beach, where I put my bare feet and hands into the surf and felt like I cleansed months of antibacterial disinfectant — the cold saltwater a salve for all the compulsive handwashing and my chapped psyche. For moments, I almost felt free.

When I was maybe six — seven — eight years old on Liberty Street in San Francisco, I felt a kind of freedom. Probably too much for that age — what would now be called unsupervised. It was more of a norm then. On rooftops four stories up, hopping over backyard fences, roaming blocks and blocks away from home.

I knew the inside of every Victorian on our post-WWII block. From the Scottish Catholic Callaghans next door and their ten kids who went to Most Holy Redeemer and wore uniforms and whose house always smelled like haggis and cabbage. Across the street, the Franz's, who had escaped the Nazis. Their grandson, Robert from London, who visited during the summertime and spoke with a British accent.

The Azevedos — the nightclub singer dad who spoke Spanish, slept late and walked around in boxer shorts, and his Irish wife, Molly, who wore colorful muumuus. And their beautiful children — two girls who all the boys had crushes on. The older one won dance prizes on American Bandstand; the younger one, a singer just like her dad; and two boys who all the girls had crushes on.

The Puerto Rican family down the street were cousins of the SF Giant's first baseman, Orlando Cepeda, who played basketball with the kids when he visited and once brought over Willie Mays. The Czechoslovakian single mom with her daughter, a classmate who had long braids and only three fingers on each hand from thalidomide. I remember holding her hand during folk dancing in school and trying not to notice. The German Lutheran Werths, who took me to church, where I sang O Tannenbaum in German — much to my Jewish father's dismay. My *shiksa* mother thought it was hilarious.

I was always going to church, believing I needed to be redeemed and save my family from hell and the fire that burned forever. That was June Callaghan's influence. "Yer father's a Jew; you can tell by his nose. Yer gonna go ta hell." Obsessed with rosaries, I stole one from June Callaghan's older sister Marie's dresser. Marie never noticed, maybe because she had moved on to the making-out-with-boys stage. Patsy Callaghan and I would spy on Marie and her beaus kissing on the living room couch through a keyhole.

There was Linda Avila — I think her father was Spanish. One day, she poured catsup on her younger sister in the basement and made me cry when she told me it was blood, and her sister was dead. And the Irish Kilkarneys at the corner of Liberty and Castro Street. The older boy hung out with Eddy Mullens, who took me up to their fort on Billy Goat Hill and showed me how to play strip poker when I was eight.

I don't remember the name of the people who lived in the house where the parents were never home — also on Castro near Liberty. Where all the big kids gyrated to 45 rpm records and made out all over the house after school. Where Denise Choroski and I jumped on the double bed in what must have been the parents' bedroom. One of the older boys took Denise and me down to the basement once and showed us a dead kitty in the freezer. We both screamed. He later joined a gang and was arrested for murder.

Frankie and his parents lived on the corner. He was from the deep South and always said, "Bless your little pea pickin' heart," which my Dad said was like Ernie Ford.

I often walked home after school with Maria Santiago, whose tongue click-clicked when she talked about her Grandma Guadalupe from Mexico who had recently died. Maria opened the door to her flat with a key she wore around her neck. Once, she led me down a dark hallway to a framed photograph of her Grandma hanging on the wall. She looked like Snow White, encased in glass with radiant blue eyes, rose tint around her lips and cheeks, and a yellow glow around her dark hair. Maria told me to watch for the eyes in the photo to move — that was how her grandmother would speak to her from the beyond. We waited and waited, and when I finally saw the eyes move, chills ran down my arms. I figured Grandma Guadalupe must be a saint.

I went to Most Holy Redeemer Church with Patsy Callaghan and read the story of Saint Bernadette in her Catechism book so many times I knew it by heart. *Saint Bernadette of Lourdes, who was downtrodden, poor and sickly, who went back and back to the Grotto to see the vision every day, even when no one believed her.* I knew all the facts about the saints: how long they had been buried before their bodies were discovered, always in miraculously preserved condition years later. I knew how beautiful they were and how much God loved them. I lengthened my name to Claudia Denise Ann Marie Sarah Bernadette Kolsch to keep myself from going to hell. But I had never heard anything about moving eyes.

I also went to church with the Cassadys, who were Unitarian. Their daughter Nan became my best friend. Her father, who always had neighbors over to discuss politics, was wrongfully accused of being a Communist. Her mother let us help make blackberry pies from scratch. Nan and I always got into trouble — mostly for laughing. We burst out giggling when Mrs. Cassady pointed out the artistic aspects of nude bodies in paintings and couldn't keep ourselves from cracking up in church.

The Cassadys lived next door to the French Trelauns, who I didn't know because they didn't have little kids. Sometimes I played with Fern Karpilow, a classmate who lived around the corner. Her parents were artists. Fern had little sisters, and I watched Fern's mother like a hawk to learn how to change diapers. She was always teaching us things. Their house always smelled sweet — like crayons and apples. They were Jewish from Brooklyn, New York — just like my Gram.

I babysat for the ballet dancers who lived in a flat on the corner of Liberty and Castro Street. I imagined they were Russian because my ballet teacher, Mrs. Parks at The Academy of Ballet, said Russians were the best dancers — but I don't think the couple on the corner were really Russian. I would steal cookies from their cookie jar while their infant slept. I didn't babysit long — just while the parents went to the store. I always seemed to be babysitting, although how anyone could leave an infant with an eight or nine-year-old — even for ten minutes — is beyond me.

The red house three houses down from us was where beatnik families moved in and out. I got my first kiss from Matt Stahl when I was six or seven years old, up in my parents' walk-in closet when his mother and mine were downstairs having coffee. When the Stahls moved out of the red house, the Hilders moved in. I played with the Hilder children, whose parents were permissive and didn't make their toddler Julia wear a diaper. The Hilders were really worried about a nuclear war and introduced me to Peter Paul and Mary — who became my new religion after I decided Christ was a hoax like Santa Claus and rosaries were just glass beads. During nuclear drills, when we hid under our desks at school around the time of the Cuban Missile Crisis, the Hilders and PP&M's songs seemed to make more sense.

After my Tennessee Valley walk, I started thinking about all this — trying to remember a time when I felt free — but what occurred to me was all the immigrants I grew up with in San Francisco. I remember my Dad talking about his whole *mespucha*, his family, and how he came from a long line of Russian peasants who fled pogroms. He said even in his generation in San Francisco's Jewish Fillmore District, the buddies he went to school with were Italians, Irish, Jews, Greeks, Negros … All sorts of ethnic names — in his generation — and mine.

We are a nation of immigrants. And as difficult as my childhood may have been at times, I miss the tapestry of Liberty Street, as good and free and refreshing as sinking my toes into the cold saltwater at the Tennessee Valley beach.

# Bird and Beckett Bookstore San Francisco

It's been too long
since I've visited,
a crammed confabulation
of living and ghosted writers,
still chattering away their thoughts
through whiffs of inked fonts.

Pound and Housman huddle
under the blistered windowsill,
where flies lie posed in *savasana*,
eternal rest
after skittering a few days
through the stacks.

And above those indignant teachers
who, when I don't take them
to the checkout counter,
will cuff my unschooled hand,
I see a stuffed pine box
with its dozens of little ones
straining for new life,
oblivious to their epitaph
carved with a felt pen:

"Chapbooks,
if not otherwise marked,
three dollars."

# Dog Path at Fort Funston, San Francisco

This modern wooden deck, hanging
over blue steel water,
will turn to driftwood
like those WWII bunkers,
hunkered down the path,
blood-rusting in fits of Golden
Gate Bridge International Orange,
like the last bank swallows
nesting below in sandstone.
The ocean thrums its goatskin
elegy to white noise
slicing the sky from SFO.

Lexie's breath stinks like dog,
which she is, gray and chesty.
Her black nails quickly rip a hole
in my journal. She wants to know
what I'm doing here,
dogless. Her owner pushes an empty
stroller, the baby strapped to her back.
Then they are gone, exploring
the carpet of pesky ice plant,
its bitter figs.

We are all confused.

# Sunday at the Civic Center

The day is hot, the rummagers are out.
Backpacks, trash cans, paper sacks, purses:
the hidden gold, such as it is,
must be extracted. These are the poor who are always with us,
who would do better to invest in pricey health care
than in the latest smart phone —
so argues the physician-turned-politician,
whose idea of the commonweal is a massive tax cut
at the behest of the super-rich swelling his war chest.

The rummagers, cutting their own deals, dig deep
for something that will make their day, their night,
week after week, month after month, year after —
Breaking news: Legislator in church rejects
"I am my brother's keeper" as a non-starter, texts
his caucus to stand firm against "spendthrift libtards."
I wonder if members of the caucus at the Civic Center

know the magnitude of what they're up against.
If they don't, I'm certainly not the one to enlighten them,
gripping my white bag of legal meds that in other hands
would be sure to disappoint — just one more non-starter
passing through, digging deep against the dark *mishegas*
of misinformation and civic disdain... But lookie here:
a tee that says — I kid you not — "LUX ET VERITAS."

The improbable is everywhere.

## Past 60

Higher and higher, the cable car ascends the tallest hill
and I know what the first-timers don't: after the crest —
the precipitous plunge, steep as death. But first, the charming
restaurants and cafes, and no end of handsome,
obscenely-priced houses, shuttered to the plum trees
brightening the streets. Higher and higher,
camera phones framing the view, all of them
useless once we peak and roll over the edge
and gather speed, the fine line between excitement and danger
obliterated, the brakeman tugging fiercely the worn
brass of his handle — almost in desperation —
every part of his body a form of applied force.
Though it feels like a downrush to oblivion
with all the odds against him, no one would call it heroic.
Yet it's impressive how he's doing his best to keep us
intact as well as entertained, slow us down,
keep us on track: the way of his work day.
Which for me now — I got here so fast — is every day.

# Accumulated Knowledge

I'd seen her at various art scenes, silk scarves and retro dresses
her trademarks, arm candy for a local politician. But when she
        asked me
to join her for a drink I didn't hesitate. How could I resist a bar
        called Toronado,
like the first ride I ever bought, inky blue muscle car with a
        Super Rocket V8?
In the subaqueous blue light of the back room, we were
        turbocharged
on microbrews — names like Crush Town and Divine Smite
        and Underworld Dreams,
and one called Accumulated Knowledge (exhilarating bouquet,
slightly sour finish) — and by the time Lester Bowie's Brass
        Fantasy
horned in on the conversation with "I Only Have Eyes for You,"
I offered my eyes, then my hand. When you slow dance with a
        near stranger,
the two of you as beautifully woozy as the jazz men's mutes,
        there can be
a lot of what an old friend calls "incredible bingo." We turned
in slowest circles, warm cheek to warm cheek, and as Lester's
        *wah wah*
more than matched the funky little ferment of Infinity Beach
(tropical citrusy with a touch of grapefruit zest), we began our
        ascent
of Mount Remarkable, no need for legs or feet. Then we kissed
— once, lightly, on the lips. I asked her if that was okay and she
said more than okay, and don't ask me how I ended up spread-
        eagled on her bed
while she smoked a clove cigarette and read aloud to me.
Cortázar's "Your Most Profound Skin" played out his own
        slow dance

in an Argentine bed, his lover's back "against a sail of white
        sheets"
as the two of them traveled "around the day in eighty worlds."
That night we needed only one world, a geography without
        jeopardy,
no terra incognita where dragons be. It was the world
of the next morning (runny eggs, coffee black and scalding)
where I learned of the deadbeat dad, the bitter mother on food
        stamps,
the little sister caught in the revolving door of the psych ward.
Older brother, ex-Marine, refused to talk, on his wrist a black
        metal band
engraved with his buddy's name and the letters "K.I.A."
Her city supervisor, twenty years her senior, kept her in a
        leather corset
and, whenever she was about to come, would press his hand
across her mouth. Then he'd finish by giving her a facial.
Her pallor, which I had complimented her on and she
        demurred,
calling herself "wan," was one sign of a blood disorder
that had her doctors worried she wouldn't live to see thirty.
She divulged all this to me with a stupefying aplomb, the same
dimpled smile as when she offered marmalade for my scone.
I would like to say we were drunk in love, and went on to see
the better side of thirty — and forty and fifty. I would like to
say any number of things I wish were true. Don't ask me what
        happened
to the Toronado, both car and bar, or slow dancing to slow jazz
while time and its terrors take a back seat. Or how the night
and the day will take turns moving us, whether tenderly or
        gingerly,
around a black and blue room someone named the world.

# Earth Is a Fickle Dancer

At the Academy of Sciences in San Francisco,
there is a fluid map of the world
where one can spin the silver toggle
with a finger, watch familiar continents
swim like fish round a globe
I thought reliable.

Once, a single vast ocean
we now call *Panthalassa*
surrounded the super-continent *Pangea*
in the southern hemisphere,
this restless Earth always moving,
tectonic plates cavorting:
the Americas thrown from Africa,
India a leaping dancer thrust
at the immovable body of the Himalayas,
the shifting floor between California
and the Appalachians flooded
with new seas.

Inch the dial one million years,
not much changes — a new isthmus here,
a new mountain there. But spin
the silver disk like the six-year old
who muscles his way in between
my torso and the luminous map
saying, *Let me see! Let me see!*
and the world reveals itself
as the Flamenco dancer it is:
the hem of her dress bunched
in hand like the Alps,
toe of her boot spinning

my leaden feet nimble,
oceans flooding into the breach
of Gibraltar with one blink
of her Mediterranean eyes.

# Something to Live For

*San Francisco Giants Stadium*

My Freudian brain is a baseball hawker
selling desire, peanuts and home runs
to drunken crowds in the bleachers of the mind.
Cracker Jacks, whisky, cigars — it's all good, man,
fluorescent smile selling
this *Id* and *Ego* battle
for the Holy Grail
at the bottom of the 9th when the bases are loaded
and you're down by three and if you could only hit that long
ball,
that one long-shot poem,
past the grasping mitt of the *Superego*
with its belief in limits and the unassailable height
of the middle field wall where this wanna-be *Superman*
leaps with agile grace, one spiked shoe clawing up the green
wood to take back what should be yours ... but look!
The scuffed white hardball of your deepest dream just flew
not only over the first wall and that last-gasp mitt,
but over the ample bellied fireman with his bucket of beer
waiting to get his meaty paw on this round icon of perfect
desire
— like your therapist, the last stand
between you and the world —
as the home run finally sails past the last banner
and you've won, finally,
after all these years.
Only to watch your great achievement fall
into the unconscious bay
where the mind's little clean-up crew
circles the Freudian waters
outside Giants stadium
in tiny yellow and red kayaks,

gawkers praying for just one grand slam souvenir,
like this one,
to fall from the sky,
land in hand just like the pros.
You cradle the poem home,
pop open a beer,
praise the gods.

# In Ancient October

Ochre's small plank

            of moon-lit

resemblance      ghost  fire warming

       knuckles and bones

then a brief loss,

  waffled      shadow releases

        thistles by moonlight

Chevron wall

        this year's vestments

under stars'

      amplitude

sparks fall's recluse omens

       how the world

is a stranger

    its rags even torn

       under stone's notice

tindered wet notion

in tinctures  of color

edged by coastal fog

we save

what we can: foster

the leave's  cold  history

# Opening Night at the Opera House

Major donors dine under City Hall's Rotunda.
This is the must-see-and-be-seen occasion.
Men in white tie, tails or tuxedos.
Women in long dresses, furs or feather boas,
wearing jewelry from the family vaults.

It's September, and the weather is always hot
for the first party of the new season —
Opening Night at the San Francisco
War Memorial Opera House.

The police are out in force —
to stop the traffic,
to protect the rich and famous.
Patrons in groups cross the street
and very slowly find their seats.
A brief welcome and reminder
"Please — No Photographs or Recordings."

The conductor enters, bows to the audience,
picks up the baton. A drum roll.
Patrons struggle to their feet.
Some try to sing the National Anthem.

A curtain emblazoned with kimonos rises.
The scenery Japanese.
In the background colorful ribbons.

Lieutenant Benjamin Franklin Pinkerton sings.
He's the tenor who takes advantage of our heroine.
We finally meet her as she marries him.
Poor little Cho-Cho-San, Madama Butterfly.

They declare their love in a beautiful duet.

I hope you brought a box of Kleenex —
the music is glorious, the ending sad.

The party continues during intermissions.
Cell phones in one hand, champagne in the other.
Patrons stand on the Opera House steps,
everyone elegant in evening dress.
They chat and smile and sweat.

Then, like a well-trained Opera Chorus,
they lift their heads and sniff the air
"The fog is coming!  I can smell it!"

We're back to normal.
Cold, gray and overcast.

# Movie Night at the Symphony

The screen hangs above the orchestra.
*West Side Story* tonight.
*Batman* and *Amadeus* are coming next.
In the summer, *Harry Potter.*

The ushers step up the pace,
as they give directions and answer questions.
"You may bring your wine in
if the cup has a lid."
"The restrooms are down the stairs.
Ladies to the right, Gents to the left."
"Yes, there is an intermission."
"Your seat is on the other side."

The warning bells sound.
"Take your seats, and
Please, Please, Please
put your cell phones away!"

The orchestra tunes — noisy dissonant sounds.
Musicians stand as the conductor comes on stage.
She bows, picks up her baton
and makes eye contact with the musicians.
The lights go down.

The Sharks snap their fingers
We are in New York City in glorious Technicolor.
Here come the Jets.
The police know there's going to be a rumble
Young love is sweet and pure
but totally forbidden.

It's *Romeo and Juliet* in modern dress —
dancing, singing, with the same fatal flaw.
Cross the line and you are in trouble.

# San Francisco Told Me to Write You a Letter

1.

do you know
that i walk these streets downtown
expecting to run into you
expecting that you would be waiting
in the park that i chose to walk through
by the hummingbirds
by the man in rags and bones
that finished the cigarette that i started
i expect magic
to be able to win out over whatever it is that's working against it
i expect my kiss
to be returned
but even if i knew it wouldn't be
i would try anyway
i would try
and then i would try

do you know that i am in love
do you know that i have always been in love
do you know that i don't know you
do you know that i've dreamt of your skin since i was a child
and that when i saw you for the second time
it was as if i woke up from a dream
i have been sleeping
but i just woke up
i am awake
but i haven't stopped dreaming

do you know that i would wait
but that i can't wait
so i am here

on your doorstep
i am naked
even though my clothes are on
i am naked
as the day we were born
do you know
that i will hurt you
do you know that you will hurt me
does it matter how bad we might make each other feel
if we can make each other feel this good

2.

the creases of your problems
fit perfectly
into the folds of my jacket

3.

dreams
that fall by the wayside
stars
that crinkle in your hand
as you kiss me
in a puff of smoke
and suddenly
disappear

4.

i did not really write this
i have not begun to write
except on the inside of your palm
my number
and in the sky
the music
this day

tonight
and the sun after it has set
the gentle graves
that these tiny deaths have to offer

where you are going

sometimes i figure it's just me
sometimes i admit
i don't know what that means
sometimes i pass your apartment
on the way home
not really on the way home
i pretend to text you that i'm here
and that i'll wait
i don't know what it means
to pretend to wait
but that's what i'm doing

5.

the sun is just gonna bury itself one day
and my body
won't even know
where my heart is

6.

missed calls
and sacred texts
i'm kind of everywhere
i don't know what this button does
but of course i'm going to push it
these are the hands i was given
and i have not yet forgotten
the face of my father

the way i became liquid
when you touched me
and stone
when you didn't
this fragile land that we all walk on
as if it weren't about to break
the amount of time you let it ring
before they will charge you
for that call

you are a drunken butterfly
and i feel the flutter
as you fly past
aware
unaware
of the things your wings
set into motion

7.

walking treetops to get to you
i remember
the rain
sweaty streets
not having a choice
and choosing anyway

8.

the sun broke through finally
just as everyone already left
and we lay there
in the park
not saying anything
your hair spilling onto the grass
a reservoir of knowledge

inside the palm of your hand
that tiny jewel the man from the gas station gave you
i liked the way he didn't say anything
he just gave it to you
as we left you turned around
and asked if it could tell the future
he said "anyone can tell the future
but that doesn't mean it will listen"

9.

there are moments like these
where i could whisper
so quietly
that even god couldn't hear us

10.

the park
was just as you left it
the ice cream soundtrack
the cigarette butts
blooming
the crooked nose guy
with the hello kitty backpack
walking backwards
around the poplar tree
the thoughts
that collected
right at the base of the slope
where we would lay
after rolling down the hill
we were spinning
and we were so high
that it didn't seem
like there would be a way to get down

we finally made it
but sometimes i wish we hadn't

11.

if i could,
i would keep the memories  i want
and forget the ones  i don't.
but since i can't,
i'll just keep them all.

# 710 Ashbury, 1967

*For Gene Anthony*

The photographer hangs out on Haight Street,
entranced by youths in beads
and braless girls in lace and feathers
who weave flowers in their hair.
He smokes weed with his subjects
and taps his foot to the beat
of Jimi, Janis and the Jefferson Airplane.

He has told his agent not to call him:
"No more dogs, flags, wine labels,
politicians or corporate portraits."
In his office in New York
the agent paces. He's apoplectic,
so many clients waiting.
His guy in San Francisco is a flake —

lugging his camera bag up Ashbury,
where nothing is more important
than Jerry Garcia in his Uncle Sam hat
and Phil Lesh with a golf club.
The photographer rings the bell at 710,
tells the Dead where to stand,
and the world snaps into place.

# András Schiff Plays Bach's English Suites

*Louise M. Davies Symphony Hall*

How does it happen
that a soft rain begins
on an April afternoon
in the symphony hall, filling
the air with points of light
that flit and flicker
with the pianist's fingers?

I walk in that rain
without hat or umbrella,
marveling that it falls
from nowhere, not a cloud
to be seen, a miracle of sorts.
I climb a small hill,
having no idea where I am,

and wonder where all
the wildflowers came from —
sun cups and fire poppies,
mountain irises, bluebells —
such a profusion of colors,
and where they go
when the music fades.

# The Bar at the End of Some Other Road

Kind of place nobody's ever walked in for the soup.
You order the soup. Barkeep thinks he's famous and has
Bottle caps for eyelids and a girlfriend who cuts
His hair so when track lights flick, looks like
Broken glass rained on his head.

Place where it feels like a fight's always about to
Break out and you're in the middle.
Combustion, then silence oomphs like a blanket over a fire,
Boom from the back room like a flat tire, you doing eighty.
Kind of place lobster traps give up, hang a hundred miles
From the sea on the cork ceiling, fish nets limp on the walls.
If you stare too long at the baseball game on TV
You might go blind, a risk you'll have to take.

Where nobody talks to you and when they do
They stare straight ahead, like now with this girl,
Can't tell for sure if she's pretty or a girl, and she goes,
You new in town? Like she means it. Says
She's never seen you in here, which is
One true thing you both have in common.

Kind of place a girl like that gives you her name
And wind picks up and you see corn silos for days
And trucks, and dogs that would drag her out of
A burning car if they have to, which you can understand,
You might do the same, the least you could do. Now her name
Comes back: Elaine. Definitely rhymes with Elaine.

She asks who's winning. She means the game, but
You know better. The pearlescent white
Buttons on her cowboy shirt gleam like her perfect teeth,
The one thing perfect in this kind of place,
Where a bowl of soup is nothing you should count on.

# Sing-Along Messiah

Is the point to bloom?
Send your sweetness out on the air. Open your petals.
Call to the bees. Lean toward the sun balancing on your tiptoes.
Duet with the rain.

Or is the point to fruit and seed?
Curl yourself into a fertile ball.
Wrap your missives to the future in lemon flesh and thorns
or into maple wings, as sparrows fly west
with your seeds in their bellies.

Or is the point to fade and die into fertilizing compost?
Drop crimson leaves. Sustain the next generation of worms
and lichen with decay. Rattle rhythmic seed pods in the wind.

Or is the point to do it all again?
Come back the next season.
Dance with the daughters of last year's bees.
Scatter seeds, wait with tubers, reawaken.
Send sweet sap up your veins.

Or is the point to tango with the universe?
Feel the energy. Give weight.
Sing your part of the Messiah.
Laugh and run as hard as you can.
Fist bump the sun.
Swing in rainforests.
Spin around the earth and moon.
Hallelujah!

# Tree #143

I.

In the city, even the trees
have unique identifying numbers.
Yesterday, a Monterey pine,
three feet across at its trunk,
was cut down,
trunk left lying in pieces,
too big for the chipper.
The stump golden in the sunshine,
damp and smelling of turpentine.

II.

They are at it again next week,
cutting down more trees,
chainsaws whine, harsh as dental drills.
What they do now can never be undone.
I watch a slow motion car crash,
bodies piled.

And yet, when they are done,
on this small hill,
my views of Pacific Ocean breakers,
quartz sand flashes of Outer Sunset,
will be grander,
my vision greater and clearer.

I am cut in half.

## Mount Sutro Tower

A Colossus of Rhodes lighthouse
signals through mist,
leading technology traders into our valleys.
Rusted remnant of the steel age —
when will our earthquakes crumple your length
onto the steep hillside, eucalyptus groves,
and deserted Nike Missile Command?

Are you a demon gate — blinking coordinates
to summon those who will scatter this world?
Sundial gnomon of the city, cosmic tuning fork,
ancient god with a clipper ship crown?

What is snared in the metallic webs
strung between your long bones?
Industrial dream catcher,
commune with the construction cranes
as sleeping fog slips through your armatures.

# San Francisco, 14th Avenue

Back from coffee, electric car silent,
I always slow in the middle
of the one-way road looking over
Outer Sunset and the Pacific Ocean.

I search the far horizon
for the jagged teeth of the Farallons.
A sailboat perches on teal blue water
where trawlers fish at night.

Cloudy mornings catch a current's silver edge,
sky ribbons of smoke gray, pewter, indigo.
White caps churn the sea,
the hush of wave-crash.

The expanse of ocean
is in perpetual conversation
with the mutable sky.

In unexpected urban quiet
I pause on the narrow overlook —
thirsty for salt air and freedom.

## Ballet Practice

Rain in San Francisco
coming down in buckets.
My car inching
toward another
intersection on Franklin —
a slow prowl toward our fate.
I've been at the same stoplight,
it seems, for 1000 years,
but Mozart is on the radio;
people outside
are pushing black umbrellas up toward
the sky, while
inside a glass building
across the street
bodies fly through the air
like finches and leaves.

# Questions for Michael after the Fact

Did you wear boots?
Anything in your pockets?
Which tattoo was the one that identified you?
How long had it been since you'd visited her?
How long were you in the water?
Had you held anything delicate that day?
Did you take BART then walk?
Did you pretend you were a tourist?
Was it too bright?
Was it a Wednesday?
What was the last piece of fruit you bit into?
Did you remember shelling peas on her back patio?
Did you remember building your sister a fence?
What did you eat before you left?
Nothing?  Did you think you could fly?
Why just past the mid-span?
What was your last thought?
Did you know your body would float
all the way to Angel Island?

# Dancing at Heron's Head

A place to ponder, an enviable solitude
in these times of viral terror and fear.
Saltwater tidal marshes along the Bay
with birds, waves and friendly dogs
amid a tranquil healing silence.

I hear a sandpipers' chorale.
Faint brightness from a single note,
stretching into two more.
Sounds from an avian bagpipe
floating on a hesitant breeze.

Along a sliver of rocky beach —
a fling of speckled brown sandpipers
with athletic loping strides,
and delicate dancers' steps —
performing a glissade on the sands.

They pirouette on long black legs,
stopping to ferret out cockles and worms
with curved pincer black beaks —
fluttering as the tide moves out
into a feathered arabesque.

# Rush Hour

How can it be, the mother scolding
her five-year-old daughter for not listening to her
while the three of them sit on the ground
in the Montgomery Street BART station —
the woman, the girl, the infant —
their red Carl's Junior box filled with loose change.
How can it be, the daughter whimpering, her head lowered
as though her mother had just scolded her
in the living room of their apartment,
the TV blaring the Five O'Clock News.
How can it be, the infant wrapped up in a pink blanket,
asleep in her mother's arms,
while the rain drips into a puddle inches from her head.
How can it be, this, the life we have chosen:
to rush home after seeing this,
to walk through the front door,
to sit down at the kitchen table,
to eat. This, after the mother,
with all the strength in her tiny voice:
*It's time, Cathy, for a time-out.*

# Reverie

During lunch at Hunan Home's,
scallops in black bean sauce,
sizzling rice that seems to quiet us,
you say, *We should have gotten married*,
words that fill us, then make us hungry,
not that we would have been good together
but for a few moments, we share our longing,
the way the conductor walked up and down
the train this morning, advising passengers
how to fulfill their goals and they listened,
or the way the big oak stood over Horse Mountain
and you used to run up to it to watch
the colts run by those winter afternoons.
*Timing was against us*, I say —
call it your anger after a failed marriage
or my fear that we were getting too close —
even as the horses walked by your window
and we listened to Chopin Sunday mornings
eating pancakes filled with blackberries from your garden.

## Earthquake, 5 A.M.

Temblor wakes me with a kiss.
On the other side of the wall,
a whirring of water.
I open thin blinds to calla lilies,
belladonna, the garden of early
morning light.

After the earthquake
the neighborhood dogs howl,
then a silence
that wraps the morning.

## Mahler on Race Day

*"I shall soar upwards:*
*To the light which no eye has penetrated!"*
*— Gustav Mahler*

In concert black, we carry two cellos
to the N-Judah streetcar
on Bay to Breakers Sunday
to play Mahler's Second Symphony.
We take seats in the front of the train
next to a unicorn, a dragonfly,
runners in rainbow tutus,
and a caveman with a leopard Santa Claus Hat.

Erik's tuxedo, bow tie and hot pink cummerbund —
well, everybody's in costume.
We sit across from a furry gray cat
and an angel with a red, white and blue halo.

To my left, a couple holding hands
and wearing the medals they got
when they crossed the finish line.
She's dressed like a bumblebee,
fuzzy antennas waving from her headband.
He carries a bouquet of larger-than-life sunflowers.

More people board the streetcar —
a three-eyed alien, a troll with pink hair,
human-size mice and bunnies.
A leopard with a fanny pack
and a six pack.

A woman who flew in from Boston
tells me the Bay to Breakers is her 73rd birthday party.
We invite her to the Mahler concert.

She started piano lessons at age 66 —
no mother to tell her
the piano won't fit in her house.

A family of bumblebees climbs into the streetcar
with black antennas and black tutus.
One of them tells me the wings
helped her up the Hayes Street hill.
Standing in the aisle,
butterfly hats, butterfly wings, butterflies.

A cello isn't out of place in this crowd.
I invite a butterfly to the concert,
but she prefers early music.
I tell her we played Beethoven's Ninth Symphony last year.
"Beethoven? That's hardly early music!"

A bear in a fuzzy costume
says that Mahler is so much better
than the new music concert he heard last weekend —
sirens and pots and pans.
The rainbow caterpillar agrees.
"Mahler has melody, chord structure, immaculate timing
and thundering beauty."

Entering the streetcar —
metallic space cylinder.
Svelte runner in orange neon shorts
and rainbow snake earrings.

Bay to Breakers — 7.46 miles,
a marathon up and down San Francisco hills
from the Bay Bridge to the Pacific Ocean.
Mahler, quite a workout —
27 pages in the cello part.
*Allegro maestoso* at the starting gate.

My teacher's advice:
"At the downbeat, play as fast as you can.
Keep running!"

At Van Ness Station, exit the streetcar.
Up the stairs, down the street, cross the race at Hayes.
Traffic signals help, as we weave two cellos
between the tutus.

A few minutes before the call,
we find the side door to the Herbst Theatre
and a friend who plays French horn for the San Francisco Ballet.
Bill says, "Mahler's Second Symphony at the Herbst Theatre?
Good for you! But is the building
large enough to hold that piece?"

Curtain, conductor, start.
It's under my fingers,
and I keep intense focus as I play.
Waves of beauty and mystery.
The soprano soloist was one of the sent-down children
during the Cultural Revolution in China.
She sang to keep herself sane,
then emigrated across the Pacific to study opera.
The mezzo, a Southern Belle, with honey voice
and tango flowers in her hair,
would do herself honors at Mardi Gras.

It's a hauntingly beautiful and mystical piece,
from the opening run
to our standing ovation.
After the applause,
after "we really did this thing,"
in the aura of post-concert afterglow,
time to take cellos back to the Outer Sunset.

On the streetcar, we sit inside
a hive of bumblebees.
A butterfly takes our photograph —
tuxedo and concert black, holding cellos.
For the next week, Mahler,
a fat moon and rainbow tutus in my dreams.

# Ultra-Body over the Mountain

So Larry says to the impromptu dancer, this one is in eleven. I'd like to see what you do with it. He's playing silver flute with a trio of jazz musicians at Union Square, high notes fluttering through a curtain of butterflies, musical nectar flying from the piano and fretless bass. She has already taken over the open space in front of the stage, smiling coyly like a geisha, winking behind her paper umbrella.

The dancer spins out of a time warp, waving peacock feathers. Black slinky pants gyrating like a snake. So thin she does not need her pink leopard bra, so she tosses it to the audience. She whirls like a dervish, a helicopter, a typhoon, her long black hair flying under a straw hat edged with a brown ribbon. The ribbon, the edge of a solar system. Her turquoise glass bead earrings orbiting like planets on a belly dancer's belt. Arc of sun shining on silver, spraying light.

Piano, flute and bass begin riffing "Ultra-Body over the Mountain." Larry's tune. The dancer, maybe Japanese, way over the hill. Arms flying, leg kicked over her shoulder. She's a unicorn leaping through time. After the rippling cadences of the flute solo, she knows the applause are for her. She opens her arms to the crowd, blows kisses to the audience.

A homeless man in bright green shorts orbits the square, sweetly happy for these few moments. His hands remember the trumpet he used to play, his childhood friend's conga drum. The bass improvisation is floating into an African dance, tribal rhythms swaying his legs and back. He leaves the lunch someone gave him on the stage. He has to keep dancing. No roof over his memories, an ocean of sky, floating with boat-shaped clouds.

A circular wind from the ocean is spinning across the stage. The Japanese dancer has become a unicorn. She almost smiles. A shower of glass beads whirls around her, the planets of a tiny universe, with meteor showers burning a path through the stars. Her stars.

The unicorn spins through time, her long Japanese hair flying in the wind. Almost a pirouette, as much as the concrete will allow. Over the mountain, maybe a moon, maybe a sun. Perhaps a butterfly. The tune climbs the mountain — weaving and winding to its slinky final chord. The butterfly bows, deep diva, face to the floor, arms flying to the moon, to the moon, to the moon.

## The Sky away from Here

Somewhere, the moon turned copper.
Druids circled Stonehenge in amber robes.
My astronomy professor was on his balcony with a telescope.
I was in San Francisco, under a thick cloud cover.

In the sky away from here,
shadows of buffalos ran across the moon
and coyotes howled their dirge to the dark night.

In London, a coven of moon-clad women
swept their homes, cooked moon soup,
chanted the old stories,
wore moonstones.

In the Zagros Mountains,
Sufis gathered in a stone circle,
read Rumi for an oracle,
became dervishes at midnight.

In Kyoto, a geisha in Pontocho
wore a kimono painted with a silk moon,
brushed her lover with a feather.

And in the Gatsby Land of the Long Island beaches,
two lovers bathed in a tide pool
using the dark of the moon
as a cover.

In San Francisco, I entered my dreams
as the rain pounded disappointment on my window,
but in the sky away from here,
luminous tattoos

danced across the sky
and shattered into new constellations —
the buffalo, the geisha,
the feather,
a tide pool of lovers
on the far side of the moon.

# Winter Warning

Fourteen hills in the distance
rutted by erosion,
deep crevices splitting their cheeks
with knife-like precision.
Pale olive and dusky beige
for lack of rain.
Sparse, stunted shrubbery,
blemishes
on a gnome's bare bottom.

Ashen sky, lying low,
seeping heavy, damp fog
that tongues the sloping hills,
teasing the thirsty earth.

We celebrate the dry, becalmed winter,
a guilty pleasure when we know better.
We need the rain, we murmur,
tossing umbrellas to the back of the closet,
denying a hole in the ozone.

Global warming, icecap melt.
Humpty Trumpty crumbles,
oozing egg onto bald-faced liars
while polar bears forage in
in the West Wing
for Big Macs and fries.

# The Ferlinghetti School of Poetics

*"All that we see, or seem, is but a dream within a dream."*
*– Edgar Allan Poe*

I:  The dream within the dream within the dream

What is it, Ferlinghetti,
Taking star turns in my dreams?
Strolling in front of cars
Haunting alleyways, stairways,
Bars? Beating moth like flitting through
San Francisco's sex fraught avenues? In North Beach
Where XXX marks art and
Nasty commerce collide, intersect Columbus,
Telegraph Hill, Jack Kerouac Way.
You are fog whispering in from the sea
On another sunny day.

"There's a breathless hush on the freeway tonight,
Beyond the ledges of concrete / Restaurants fall into dreams
With candlelight couples / Lost Alexandria still burns." *

Ferlinghetti's words sink, weighted
On the business end of an invisible fishing line,
Dredging last nights' dream to surface, gasping for air
Shivering like some catfish
Eyes bulging, wet lake water dripping off its scales.
The knife of memory slices open
That dream, finds me on haunted streets,
Instructing small boy:
"You gotta go to the Ferlinghetti school. It's totally rad
and completely cool."

II:   Ferlinghetti Makes an Appearance

Phantom audience shouts: "Higher! Higher!"
Egg the poets on — after all, they're not on the wire.
Higher? We spin the memory wheel until there's my father
Strolling through his own Coney Island
And there he is again winning a goldfish
The clerk hands it over fish circling in plastic bag
Big Daddy pretends
It's all for the kids.
He needed to win like that fish needed water.

III:   The Poet Reconsiders

Is the skill of life just keeping on
All the gears oiled, the doors open?
Even if the past keeps drowning and the knifed open
Dream fish still swims around?

In dream theater Ferlinghetti arrives.
Was it the Regal, the Royal or the Metreon?
I rise to make room for he who started everything
Got the wheel of poetry turning, broke
Open language, letters. Vaporized
While he drifts
Haunting my dreams.

---

*From "Wild Dreams of a New Beginning" by L. Ferlinghetti

# The Summer I Stopped Resisting and Learned to Love the Fog

Through foggy filter
steely ocean
is a grey plate

No reflection
The sun's absorbed

the entire light spectrum

into this beautiful
muted summer

# Golden Gate Bridge's 50th Anniversary Bash

Morning fog clings to Marin Headlands
like gray negligee hugs hefty hips
as we merge with other revelers
to stroll Golden Gate; no cars allowed.

We access the ramp, our destination
San Francisco, and tread the gentle
incline to the highest point, midsection
of the bridge, as an equal number
of celebrators depart the city
going north. The sun banishes fog
to the Pacific Ocean, the morning
breathes out breezes of jubilation.

Only a poet could have conceived
and built this marvel. Joseph Strauss,
chief civil engineer, was such a bard.
Class poet at university, this dreamer
made manifest his vision — a suspension
bridge with towers so tall, angels
play on its orange steel jungle gym.

Hundreds of thousands of celebrants
trudge toward the middle, thickening
with bodies. We cannot advance,
though hordes push from behind.
The crisp air thins, confusion sets in.
We are elbowed, pummeled by backpacks,
our feet trod on but all remains peaceful.
300,000 people flatten the bridge's center,
but it does not break for the Golden Gate
Bridge is imbued with the magic of poetry.

# Third Street Cowboys

I grew up in the San Francisco of Immigrants.
Color and language took a back seat to survival.
Victory garden backyards provided an arsenal
against the hunger of dock strikes.

Italians on one side, Mexicans on the other,
Maltese, Irish and Portuguese down the street.
We bought salted cod for *bacala*
from Mr. Chan at the corner grocery store.

My grandmother's Italian backyard of produce —
chard, tomatoes, zucchinis,
a canopy of fig, apple, and pear trees.
Sunday dinner chickens in the coop.

What we could not use we shared.

Anne and June, my next-door best friends,
were twin daughters of a Baptist minister
who served the Bayview District
with Alleluia praises to the Lord.

Third Street, one border of Butchertown,
was lined with slaughterhouses,
connected by train tracks —
our country's meat warehouse.

Saturday mornings with my father,
on the Third Street bridge, greeting
South American cargo ships,
watching their long-horned passengers disembark.

Cowboys with lassos and chaps
astride chestnut and black quarter horses
clopping down Third Street
leading steer to their slaughter.

The San Francisco I live in now
is occupied by citizens of
Starbucks, Peet's, or Philz.
Heads down, mesmerized by a screen.

I feel like my grandparents,
an immigrant in a strange new land —
a San Francisco barren of victory gardens,
Third Street cowboys, and Mr. Chan.

# The Colby Street Slalom Skiers

When I was eight, we lived on a cloud-kissing hill in San Francisco that descended into a bustling T- intersection. Using this backdrop for their reasoning, my parents told me I would not be getting a bike for my birthday because it was unsafe to ride on the streets near our house. As visions of a cherry-red Schwinn faded into the tangled traffic at the end of our block, I invented a remedy to my disappointment.

Organizing a group of my fellow bikeless friends, we hiked up to the top of our street. Each of us carried a metal roller skate. Looking down over our urban vista, we discussed potential courses, velocity and escape routes. Then we began our construction.

Opening our skates to their longest length, each one of us carefully positioned a flat board, 6" wide by 18" long, across our own expanded skate and firmly wedged it between the toe and heel clips. Everything was secured in place by tightening the wing nut on the underside of the thin metal skate. The finished products looked like a short-armed cross with wheels.

Sitting dead center on our boards, with our legs stretched straight in front of us, we leaned into the power of gravity and surrendered to the steep slope, using only our hands on the edges of the board to steer. Like Olympic slalom skiers, we glided over the sidewalk, weaving in and out of driveways, navigating the concrete and asphalt moguls with charmed agility. The true test of our skill was making the sharp left-hand turn into Mr. Giminani's bushes on the corner to avoid being catapulted into the heavy cross traffic at the bottom of the hill.

After earning our bruises, we all mastered the art of flying in the face of fear. I can't say the same for Mr. Giminani's bushes. Epilogue: I have never owned a bike, but as an adult, I took up hang gliding.

# Childhood

The famed seven hills of San Francisco are actually myriad: hills
and steep slopes everywhere in the seven-mile by seven-mile
square of the city. Sidewalks that are stairways. Trees and houses
clinging to ground, seemingly at 45°, climbing upward to starry
skies. Small ethnic neighborhoods sprinkled around — Russian,
Italian, Chinatown, the Black community of Fillmore Street,
the Hispanic Mission District, Gay Castro — and the Haight
Ashbury, the diverse, integrated neighborhood where I grew up
before the hippies came. Downtown, in the Financial District,
when I was a teenager, they built a new peak: the Transamerica
Pyramid, tallest building in the city, vaulting up to the sky like the
seven hills, a new eighth wonder to rival the world-famous towers
of the Golden Gate Bridge. What a marvel, what a miracle, the
city was in my childhood. Don't call it Frisco. Native-born San
Franciscans just say, The City. Living now thousands of miles away
in snow country, I miss my hometown. Such deep richness and
largeness of culture and utter beauty. San Francisco.

> steep hills, The City —
> pyramid skyscraper glows
> in my child mind's eye

# Free Ride

As a kid in San Francisco, waiting for a bus,
in morning fog, to go to school, I would see
the 6 Masonic appear magically out of what
was essentially a deep, soft cloud resting

on the earth. The bus would shoulder its way
through thick mist like a green and yellow
Triceratops, the loud hiss of its air brakes,
a breathy sound, punctuating its slow approach.

The slight ozone scent of the trolleys arcing
above would counterpoint the salty taste
of the cool air, wafting through the city
from Ocean Beach, from the Pacific.

Getting on the bus, I'd hold out the student
Muni cardboard punch card, and the driver,
big beard like a black Santa, rather than
punching out one of the 10 rides, would click

the air above my hand and card: a free trip.
He smiled huge every morning, glad to be
giving a schoolboy a boost. I bet that man
is wrangling a Muni bus up in heaven today!

# The Front Door

was a surfboard speeding forward through the '60s
except when it slammed, stopping time like granite
if not for the glass pane in the door, which let in
San Francisco's lights, the fog like gray cotton,
screeching brakes, my friend Hart's house across
Parnassus St. But the door didn't stop time. Mom
came in, said, *Hart is dead, Vin. Sorry to tell you.*
The night before, running from the police, Hart
had driven off a cliff at Land's End. A joyride
with a friend. Holy fuck. I could have stopped it
when I was on the N Judah streetcar a month before
and saw Hart with a coat hanger breaking into a VW.
I could have got off, said, *What are you up to, Hart?*
*C'mon, give it a break, buddy. Let's go get a coke.*
But the moment was past. The N Judah kept on,
the steel wheels skirling on the tracks, twisting time
into ribbons. I imagined Hart would stop stealing cars,
throw down the screwdriver. But that time, I didn't
get off the streetcar and confront my friend. There was
always time. Some time I'll do it, I'll say to Hart,
*Just stop, will ya?* But that future day was stillborn.
The taste of silver on the eyes, 9-volt batteries
on the tongue, fingertips on the hot iron smelling
like burnt toast. That logic was no damn logic. Nada.
The KFRC record on my dresser, that album I had
borrowed from Hart last year, said, *What you gonna*
*do now, chickenheart?* I pictured myself at that cliff
where Hart died, spinning that borrowed record into
the sunset air, where it would sail forever, surfing
to heaven and the future years Hart would never have.
But I didn't do that. I didn't get off that streetcar.
Moment past. Surfboard crashed. Front door closed.

# Doggie Diner, Geary and Arguello, 1969

Out of San Francisco night, the cool fog's
gray fingers caressing hills and houses,
emerged, in chef's hat and bowtie, the Dog.
A 7-foot dachshund's head in fiberglass.

Tina, my first real high school girlfriend,
and I entered through the shiny glass doors,
holding hands, both in hippie leathers, suede
vests and floppy hats, bellbottom cords.

It smelled like hog heaven, grease-laden air,
scents of amber-gold fries and sizzling thick
burgers, the sharp tang of cole slaw vinegar.
We ordered dogs slathered in chili with pickles

and mustard. The world was copacetic. Above
the diner, the Dog slowly turned, glowing like love.

# The Catch

Night game at Candlestick toward the end of its days.
June Rockwell, season ticket-holder of the so-so Giants,
has lured me out to see the wretched Cubs. First date.
When I pick her up, she asks if I've brought my glove
and I tell her I'm from the Bronx where we do everything
with our bare hands.

Thin crowd, uneventful innings, until two out in the seventh,
when Chicago's lumbering, chaw-spitting right fielder
nicks a rising heater that sails backward several sections
from our box seats into a circular gale like the twister
in *Wizard of Oz*, the ball at its apex still no real concern
twenty rows away.

And yet, in its final moments, the object of common regard
begins to beam intently, inevitably, for my patron's unarmed lap.
I? Bud Light in one hand, fully adorned bratwurst in the other,
no kidding, I refuse to panic, so the hot dog becomes at last
the missing glove, explodes like a grenade as the seamed orb
makes exceptional contact.

When, after a decent interval, I look up, June, standing now,
a Jackson Pollock of ballpark cuisine — tinsels of pork rind and
sauerkraut in her startled hair, glitter of mustard and relish from
brow to chin — says not a word, does not go to wash up,
just lowers her quivering body. The wind dies. The home team fails.
We do not speak on the drive back.

Ah, what might have been. But not for me. I'm romantic in that
other way. This way. For this night, no if-only will ever rival what
happened. Watch as we reach June's flat, she turns, caked still
with the spectacle I have made of gallantry and kisses me.
Softly, briefly, decisively. Watch the fog rise to claim her
for the perfect past.

# Wells Fargo

Hunched right behind me in Kafka's bank line,
an octogenarian with 49ers cap askew
and white stubble as old as his last floss,
grunts, *Slowest in the Western States,*
so I ask him how he knows,
and he snorts, *Don't be a smart-ass,*
informs me he's hiding from the social director
of his assisted living center, volunteers
some inside scoop on the distant tellers:
*One only does wire transfers to South America;*
*the other isn't yet trained to handle cash.*
A supervisor with the name tag "Jerry"
is cruising the crowd ready to apologize
in English, Spanish or Tagalog
for whatever no one else is sorry about.
The old dude tells him he's feeling
estranged from his capital, says,
*All I need are a couple of crisp hundreds*
*to give as Christmas tips to my barber*
*and my life coach.* Jerry offers him a Dum-Dum
and some hand sanitizer with aloe. I offer
to get him scratch paper so he can write a poem.
He mumbles:
*Roses are black,*
*my nose just bled,*
*and my balls itch,*
*so I'm not dead.*
Then he asks if we can switch places —
*Time is running out faster for me,* he says.
At which point I have to question
whether any of this actually happened,
or if it's just a talk I'm having with myself

twenty years from now,
in line for something else I think is mine,
or I want to buy,
or I've already paid for.

# At Mile Rocks

From Point Lobos, named by the Spanish
for barking seals they decided were wolves,
you can see near the breakers,
on a black lava outcrop barely above the swell,
a column, twenty feet high,
red and white stripes almost faded to bone.

Some say it's the stump of a sea-swept lighthouse
built after a steamer from Rio went down in the fog,
not by engineers, who refused, but by seamen,
their wives still roaming Land's End with flashlights,
only the base intact now,
a salt lick for pigeons and gulls.

Some say it's the work of immigrant Wu Zhao
who raised a pillar at the mouth of the Bay,
then boated out daily for months
to etch the names of forced laborers
into her squat limestone creation, until,
while carving out the character for "slave,"
she slipped and let go.

It's a nice hike over to the crusted beach
closest to Mile Rocks, along failing cliffs,
the Golden Gate Bridge at your back.
Among maze walkers and unleashed poodles,
backpackers and stockbrokers
rinsing toes in the surf, you may meet
a spent mariner staring out to sea
or share the shoreline with a woman from Kunming
who's been out to mix with ghosts,
laid joss sticks and tossed blossoms.

And you may wonder why both stories
can't be true. Why the dead
to whom sailor and stranger are paying respects
aren't your dead too.

# Why I Like Graffiti

*A personal manifesto — for Jack Hirschman*

Because we're not supposed to do it
because buildings are holy
billboards precious, walls
worth more than gold
because we're not supposed to do it
touch their buildings, climb their fences, hang like a bird
from their roofs
leave our mark

Because it's there for everyone to see
no museum guards to track you, no fish-eyed lady
collecting your entrance fee to another airless palace
of "legitimate" art no cultural dues to pay
to prove you can look and if you're young
and the wrong color and lively
you're asked to leave ushered into the street
where you belong

Because it's out there in the breathable air
framed by the sky and the hustle
curved Hebraic letters of tags
peaceful bombings
murals full-scale pieces mesmerizing fences
charm bracelets across eyesore alleys
nonviolent violence
without laying out a dime to the gods of advertising
right under the noses of the civic censors
late at night on a bicycle a backpack full of paint
art where it belongs where we can see it

Because when I look at graffiti I know what I would make
with my spray can nozzle, my paintbrush,
my broad-tipped marker
women's faces, all kinds
in repose, hilarious, tragic, divine, girls and crones
so we can see ourselves
not on the oil slicks of billboards singing
for whiskey or cigarettes or love

But floating across a vacant lot on Harrison
pressed into the abandoned walls of a brewery south of Market
high-styling an office building
meditating on the financial district, its spilled curbs
and unopened windows, on financiers, laborers
and the dispossessed
real women looking us straight
in the eye

And in spite of the aneurysms of culture
the instinct to close the door turn
up the heat and die peacefully with what I already know
graffiti makes me love the streets again:
wild horses, Malcolm X, whimsical dogs, urgent signs
kids screaming their names
because we're not supposed to do it
make this cemented world ours

# All Without Leaving Union Square

*With excerpts from an article in the SF Chronicle,*
*1/10/19, by Maggie Hoffman, Cocktail Reviewer*

Long considered a wasteland of department stores and bland
high-rise hotels Union Square has become
a hotbed of *apertivi*

Chic and hip you can bring your out-of-town relations
to elegant cocktail lounges where every night
new drinks are born!

Sprayed with tarragon oil garnished with fresh mint soothed in
pineapple syrup and wallowing in
aged pot-stilled Irish whiskey
at $72 a bottle

You can sit in candlelit corners of high-rise hotel bars
laughing over multi-layered cocktails with quirky names!

And it's 48 degrees in Union Square tonight and someone
will freeze to death holding a pint of cheap vodka
in her arms

while crushed ice is sprayed with fennel tea syrup licked
with Fernet as the bartender slicks a glass
with 18-year-old single malt scotch

and someone's head is in a trashcan
fishing for sandwich rinds and pizza crusts.

Tourist buses blare, hawkers hawk tickets to Alcatraz,
the Women in Black walk up Powell Street
on Black Friday,

hungry natives stare out from benches
as an absinthe rinse
slips stealthily over our tight and human square.

# Love Note to San Francisco

Our base in a game of tag
one foot on the city and we're safe.

The J Church, the 10 Monterey
one took me to ballet
the other brought me home.

The closed-forever Emporium
a ferris wheel on its roof
giddy in the sky over Market Street.

Childhood dioramas
standing us next to our mothers
and our best friends
bobby pins from Woolworth's
in our fly-away hair.

Now it's a playground for wealth
they take our parking places
but not our Jimmy the Butcher stories
free slices of salami for the girl who danced by.

The city is still our main game
we want it to remember us
to call us home.

The way our parents called us in to dinner
from the hide-and-seek of the streets.

## The Dawn is a Mirror of Myself

*After the painting by Lawrence Ferlinghetti, 1994*

Not just any dawn — a San Francisco dawn,
the sun blushing through the soft burn
of fog floating low over the water

between the Isle of Angels and North Beach bohemia.
It's time to tune in to a silver waltz
or something slower, to allow our bodies

what they wish most, to ease back with nowhere
but here, wings folded beneath the canvas,
sated from dreams of love and sublimity —

the whole scene a breathless hush of rose
and release — a tidal wave of it —
recorded for time.  Dawn's skin,

made of earth and heaven, warms —
is perfectly moist
to the touch.

# The Bay Was My Backyard

The little steps slick with seaweed
studded with barnacles
led to the shallow-rim mudfloor
where we rifled for starfish,
so common then,
common as the back-and-forth
sardine boats
and dared slow walks
up the dark maw of the sewer
Who would go furthest?
It all smelled, the sewer the slime
the stars sagging our pockets
half to our knees.  Honeybees
droned around us as we
laid on the green to dry among
small wild daisies with their
pink and white petals, defying
all the rules but nature's.
No I wasn't allowed off the block but was
No I wasn't allowed in the water but was
No I wasn't allowed to lie but they weren't
my rules after all. If I could've
I would've caught the first gull-clouded boat
slapping out under the bridge,
collected salt in my hair,
foghorns moaning *Don't go*

## Clouds (Selected excerpts from a longer poem)

My city whose hair is a cloud fire
Whose dreams are tumbleweeds of mist
Whose body is a ladder from barnacle to night star
Whose mouth bares the fragrance of the white-flecked sea
Whose tongue is of onyx and humming wires

My city whose streams are rock doves and parrots
Whose bright arm is a springboard for love and suicides
Whose heart is filled with winsome flowering kisses
Whose lap is a playground of canvas swings
Whose ghost stands behind them pushing them, pushing them

Up from the silver portal of heaven
Into the silver portal of heaven

    •••

White vespers.  Fog suspends, enters
smooth-coated and swift, swings
the deep bell of the bay.

The city rises into it, lips
half-open

    *Come to me voiceless as snow*
    *majestic river flowing*
    *Shape my nights*
    *Dream-float through me*
    *as the evening star shines through*
    *to find the woman there*

    *Silver melt of sorrow's opposite,*
    *brush my waiting beneath the cypress*

*cleaved and swept, perpetually*
*receiving.  Hold open your palm*
*Droplets gather fragrance from the shore*
*Torrential mist!*
*You are the poetry and the tongue*
*of my hills*

•••

The low gray sky is living.  Cool clouds loll
and roll into soft shapes — migrating bears.
Foghorns call.

Their song has two notes — a rise, a fall.
Haunting pairs that drape us
in silver-winged shawls.

We dream-walk, hesitate and stall
to feel the tingle on our skin — soft salty air
billowed from the sea over the old brick wall.

Mist floats past the steeples of Peter and Paul.
It has floated for hundreds of years.
We are the world's disintegrating dolls

let loose from red/black halls
into experience – hearts burning like flares.
The fog moves in, covers us, and dares.

•••

Foglight, there is a mystery about thee —
a silent heavenish thing
risen from the sea in waves
of ghostly wings

It is light —
the air upon the breast
is angel breath — sweet
among the shadows
of love's slant universe

# The Columbus Hotel Arcane

1.

In this old hotel where immigrants
from China, Mexico, Burma, the
Miskitos from Nicaragua, and
from the U.S.A. as well,
workers and artists, who've
come to San Francisco
and especially North Beach,
which is the zone of Chinatown,
the old Italian area of cafes
and the strip clubs on Broadway.

Exiled within exile with different
languages and get-along Hi's.
No toilets in the rooms,
kitchen stoves down the hall.
Each day I go there with a flower
of Bok Choi, that delicious
Chinese vegetable, a package
of spicy Ramen noodles,
a small pot, a knife
and a tablespoon.

I wash the Bok Choi, tearing
away the stems, lay them
on the counter beside the stove,
fill the pot half-way, cut
the Bok Choi into pieces
and put them with water
into the pot. In 7 or so
minutes I'll return to kitchen,
break the little stiff pack
of noodles over the water,

and after 3 minutes more
I'll enter the spicy powder
and bits of herbs from
two tiny packets
into the mix. And stir to
make a delicious soup.
Today, Jasmine's in
the kitchen wooden-spooning
some ground beef bits
and vegetables in a large

frying pan. She's Burmese,
talks Spanish and American
to her three children.
The other woman in the kitchen
is Maria, a Mexican. She's at
the sink. There's a striped
I believe fish in a basin she's
standing over, and when
Jasmine tells me it's
ground beef she's stirring,

I ask Maria the Mexican
what kind of fish she's cooking?
She looks perplexed, then
lifts a striped towel out of
the basin, and laughs.
We all laugh a chuckling
kind of laughter at my mistake.
But it reminds me
and, to tell a joke
I say:

"You know what's my favorite
food? — Fried shoes."
They both look quizzically
at me. "You know, fried shoes,
like in that Charlie Chaplin
movie." At the mere mention
of his name, a sunburst
of happiness fills
the faces of both
of the women.

2.

In my 36 years in this old hotel
whose name's gone from
the Tevere Hotel to
the Columbus Hotel
I've never seen such
a laughter register so
completely as to manifest
a fully human presence,
as with those women
and, for a few moments,

we all were utterly unified
and completely at home with
and even inside each other.
It wasn't the fried shoes,
it was the mention of
his name transformed them
from sluggishly moving
mamas in a terrorized
wartime of insecurity to
radiances in a radiant world.

Charlie Chaplin who I realized
then still spoke to the simple
in people, that the simple
wasn't, after all, dead
but profoundly enduring,
where the first thing
and the last thing
are the same thing
and the sounding
of the sea

of memory can
bring to the eye
a drop
of water that's
the whole sun
from the moment
it was born
to its death
at the end
of time.

# The Greta Arcane

1.

Not even the face of Garbo
in *Ninotchka* a decade after
the start of talking movies
could find its way to be a

painted mural on a wall at
Mason and Post Streets in
downtown San Francisco,
where the face of Greta

Thunberg is realized by the
Argentinian muralist Andres
Iglesias, who signs his work
with the name of Cobre.

He's caught in his image of
the teenage activist who's
won the hearts of the young
and old of the world for the

truth of her activism for the
necessary demands for the
climate changes necessary
to save the environment from

certain destruction, and her
"How dare you?!" is repeated
on the lips of teenagers and
adults allover the world, who

are duplicating her standing
before the United Nations and

insisting that the racketeers of
the globe put down their money,

begin to deal with the nature
that's choking from their greed
that's deafened them to cries
of human animals everywhere.

2.

I'm one of the 80 year-olds who
cheers that girl, for her courage
has lit up the screens of all the
computers in the world, with a

cause that's essential, which
should be addressed by those
who know the environment is
in the greatest danger of its life.

And in the heart of that young
woman who seeks no prizes,
thinks attachments of fame to
her are ridiculous absurdities,

I also see unforgettable Greta
Garbo in *Ninotchka*, a woman
of the Soviet Union, who'd have
nothing to do with capitalism's

antics, who wore a face of clear,
defiant certainty, glowing with a
truth of cause that wouldn't be
tricked or fabricated away and,

hearing that dedicated, intense
affirmation of necessary truths
in the brilliantly direct words of
Greta Tintin Eleonora Ernman

Thunberg, I'm humbled by the
quiet glory of the women of my
life, and of the world, who can,
at any apt moment of injustice,

become thunders of bluntness
facing the need to be done with
the evasions exasperating those
resonating with "How dare you?!"

# Tanforan Assembly Center
*San Bruno, 1942*

To escape the squeeze of quarters
hung with sheets for privacy,
I join hundreds circling
the racetrack, our scuffing feet
obscuring hoof prints
from race horses that used to pace
this endless oval.

Ahead, my little sister Midori
and her friend Fumiko
bend their heads close
to whisper secrets, as if still
strolling the halls of high school.
I pass our old neighbors,
Mr. and Mrs. Fujita, who shuffle
slowly with newfound leisure,
rekindling memories, sharing
the weight of worries.

I climb to the top of the grandstand,
high above day-to-day grief.
In the corner, the Shimizu brothers
roll a game of dice.
Mr. Morita meditates next to a man
stretched out asleep on a bench.

My eyes skim above the barracks
and barbed wire, follow trains
rumbling in the distance,
planes glinting overhead,
to the outline of foothills that

remind me of our San Francisco home,
only a few miles away —
beyond reach.

# Shikata Ga Nai

*Shikata ga nai*
means
It can't be helped

which translates
scour and scrub
till the smell of horse urine
is a faint memory,
cobble a table out of
scavenged fruit crates,
create a home from the stall
that is temporary shelter for
your family of six.

Pretend you don't see barbed wire
or soldiers with rifles in guard towers
when you gaze at Heart Mountain on the horizon.

*Shikata ga nai* —
a tacit agreement
to adopt the government jargon:
        relocation and internment,
                not concentration or prison camp,

to be as American as possible,
having to prove your loyalty
even though you were born here.

And when your daughter hungers to know
about your life in camp,
you giggle about the "hi-jinks girls"
and being prom queen,
a typical teenage life.

It suggests
your secret, mounting dread
each year as December 7<sup>th</sup> approaches,
even now, over sixty years later.

*Shikata ga nai* means
       End of discussion.
       I don't want to talk about it.
       There's nothing more to say.

# Gaman

*"Gaman" means to endure hardship with patience and dignity.*

It's impossible to pack
three decades of married life
in two suitcases.
How do I choose what to carry
into uncertainty?

The notice nailed
to the telephone pole
ordered us to bring bedding,
plates and utensils, clothing, told us
cameras, radios, and our dog Rusty
aren't allowed.

I'll wear my Sunday dress, hat and coat
over a couple of housedresses,
pack my grey sweater, nightgown,
unmentionables. Find room for
my Bible, our wedding portrait
and tuck in dignity, patience —
*gaman.*

# The Daily Dog Alarm

Leaping, yowling, howling, singing,
a circus of wild animals
just over our fence.

It's only four of them, but it could be a dozen.
Full force
for as long as it takes to unwind ...
or un-wind.
45 seconds later, back into the house.
Neighborhood quiet once again.

One can well imagine what sparks the ritual.
Dogs are no different than children —
at any perception of attention deficit,
"Mommy, look at me!  ME, me me!"
"Waah, he nipped me!"
"She sniffed me first!  Make her go lie down."

But far more complicated than children
when talking does no good at all
compared to a friendly scritch behind the ears.
And what canine wouldn't want to receive from both hands?
Unconditional love, that's all they want.

That's all anybody wants.

4 dogs, one wonderfully nice but harried human.
Heart of gold; she means no malice.
The problem is simple:
Not enough hands.

She tries sending them to "obedience" school
but back home, they happily retrain each other.

They're really good at that — much practice time.
They socialize exactly as dogs will
when needs are not understood.
Who needs the training more, I wonder?

Every morning, one pretty lady in her bathrobe,
tripping over furry feet, furry tails,
lots of furry faces clamoring for love.
Oblivious of her need for morning coffee.

Finally, she can stand it no more.
Out!  All of you, out!
Let the neighbors deal with it.
She has no idea.

# A Sea Change

*Certain things they should stay the way they are.*
*You ought to be able to stick them in one of those*
*big glass cases and just leave them alone.*
    *– Holden Caulfield, Catcher In The Rye*

Arms linked,  my mother and I walk up Powell Street,
laughing while Joe Selle, the San Francisco
street photographer snaps our photo, like he
always does when we shop downtown.

My mother holds a White House department store bag,
and we wear nylon stockings, white gloves, stylish hats,
voguish skirt suits, fancy heels,
our 1950's version of high fashion.

I carry a paper bag of my re-soled shoes from
Frank's shoe repair next to Bernstein's Fish Grotto,
its magnificent ship's prow jutting out on the sidewalk,
welcoming diners for a complete meal under $8.

Behind us is the Manx Hotel, built after the 1906 earthquake.
We laugh hard at something Joe Selle
says while he takes our picture
with the huge camera slung from his neck.

Joe charges $1.00 for three photos, postage included.
My mother buys so many of his photos he greets
us by name. She likes Joe, says he is a courteous
gentleman who works at an honest living.

We lunch just down the street from The City Of Paris,
at Townsends, the place Herb Caen
called the "little old ladies hangout"
to eat creamed spinach decorated with hard boiled eggs.

The Manx Hotel is now the tony Villa Florence
Bernstein's Grotto is a Walgreens, the White House
closed in the '60's, Townsends is Goorin's Hats
and the City of Paris is Neiman Marcus.

Today I walk downtown streets full of skateboarders, scooters, bikers,
Ubers, tourists carrying designer shopping bags,
security guards at stores,
techies scrolling non-stop, waiting for tall buses
to spew them at jobs.
Nobody laughs the way we did.

# For Trudy

Trudy shuffles into the pawnshop,
her head bent as if looking for something.
Her wispy grey hair trails onto a ripped sleeve,
her mouth a streak of red, her blue eyes
hinting at a face that once turned heads.

She places pocked hands on the counter,
nails ringed in black like miniature obits.
I turn to the computer to write up her usual —
a thin gold chain, knotted, lightweight, but
heavy enough for a $10 loan.

I look back at her.  She's disappeared.
Hands still on the counter,
her frail body is like a balloon losing air
she's compressed accordion-like
against the glass counter's side.

"Trudy, Trudy, wake up."
In slo-mo she rises, eyes half-mast.
Her right hand fumbles in her pocket,
in one fast movement
out comes the matted gold chain.

I put it on the scale. I know the exact weight.
I type up the ticket, go around the counter.
I place the $5 and the ticket in one pocket,
the other five ones in the other pocket.
I take $2 from my jacket and add it to her money.

"Trudy, listen, try to hold onto the money this time."
Her eyes lock onto mine.

She smiles sweetly at me.
I pat her ripped sleeve and smile back.
We both know how her day will turn out.

# North Beach Night

Neon buzz above Columbus on Columbus Day
is night's way of reminding us we are not indigenous
people trying to sleep in the Hotel Bohème but interlopers,
incredulous that beatniks have become respectable,
their portraits on bathroom walls like those of bankers
and industrialists in uptown Midwest steakhouses.
City Lights shines through the midnight haze
of fires razing the state and darkening patriarchs
taking over the globe with their towering hotels,
so unlike here where the doors use steel keys
and the stairs bear stains of shoes
that have trudged these streets in search of poetry.

# My San Francisco during the Pandemic

In a way, I miss the walk between the rickety parking garage
on Eddy Street over to my ninth-floor psychotherapy office
in the Flood Building. Scent of garlic wok fried vegetables

mingled with rotted food. There's the Tenderloin, abutting
Union Square, in one block, from single room occupancy hotels,
small grocery markets to Nordstrom and Bloomingdales. In a way,

I'm still there, navigating around the street people, checking out
the jewelry venders. I'm on the way to the recliner chair I searched
for so it would cradle my lower back. The orchids that would

have been there if I had bought them are blooming in fuchsia
and white. Cable cars turn outside the window, drowned out
by illegal street music, occasional protest marches, more

numerous now. How many times I walked up Nob Hill following
the tourists on the famous cars, turned left at California Street
to Grace, cathedral that thinks it's in Paris. Closed. But now

I amble quiet tree lined streets, even redwoods in the front yards,
visit the HP garage with a history plaque on Addison at Waverley.
It's shut me down in a way, my car in the driveway, points north

like a hound on a leash. But I'm not going there, the place I fell
on the corner of Eddy and Cyrill Magnin, lunch box, brief case,
nosediving like missiles around me. The sale rack downstairs

at Anthropologie where I got a text message from my sister
about our mother's eating less and sleeping more. The walls
of my office, their echoes of the secret gifts I listen to, the feelings

painting our atmosphere in greens and blues, with occasional red and black slashes. Is it still there? The world of my days as it shifts, shimmers, almost a mirage.

# Golden Gate Sunrise

*San Francisco, July 2014*

Thinning fog shrouds Sutro Tower,
winds a vaporous boa around the Cliff House.
A string of soaring pelicans skim silver ocean.
I stand upon stone bluff,
intrigued by wet-suited surfers straddling boards
among pulsing waves.

Defying gravity, one lanky dude
paddles to ascend swelling breaker.
Arms outstretched, he balances,
triumphantly crests muscular surge,
glides ashore through misty pink sunrise.

Joggers pound the elevated trail.
At low-tide line, I probe beached runes:
jellyfish, empty crab shell, broken sand dollars.
Salty breeze spills airborne tangles
of squabbling seagulls.

Egg yolk sun suffuses hilltops,
slides down Twin Peaks,
haloes N Judah Streetcar,
wind shaped dunes.

# The Crackling Hills

The fire is near the sea as it grows,
with animals diving in waves to swim
to anywhere for a while. Anything
to avoid the surrogate for the sun.
The sea sends fog to cool the tattered grass,
lend some modesty to the leafless trees.
Then it sends the rain, a part of itself,
to end one thing as it begins another.

Even the splendid can be ruined, the warmth
we need can be so angry it rages
and destroys as it destroys itself,
while beings glide below the sea's ceiling,
where everything is guarded by water.
We noticed all this a long time ago,
which is why we made up good and evil,
tokens for why we live and why we die.

## Land's End

Not just one night but all the nights
I've wandered here, stirring birds and
Counting waves, while the sunny moon
Kept burning holes in thoughts
I'd saved for darkened walks.

Squat ships of steel surprise
By standing on the nervous sea
As though their hearts were cork
Concealed in livid shawls
To tease the staring shore.

The late straw grasses of a
Dry season litter earth turned
Old with waiting, while torn trees
Turn from the gone sea-wind
In living fear of its return.

Implacable as litanies
The night-time water comes
To slide its seamless hands
Across the gray and sandy
Belly of its solitary love.

Deep in a catacombed cove where
Even fools would dread, the dead
Birds lie, too damp for ants, un-
Turned sand about their marbled
Eyes as though some more could happen.

Here, on the tapering brink
That ends my home, the cathedral

Size of nature weights
The soul with endlessness
Until the cries of children

Tearing meek flowers from
Their earth would seem
A peace against the terror
Of this land too long too
Close to the overwhelming sea.

# I Made Chicken Adobo for Lawrence Ferlinghetti

In the stacks of City Lights bookstore,
I wished hard to see him, Ferlinghetti.
At Golden Gate park,
I pretended every elder man was him.
Would he wear a scarf to flutter in the San Francisco wind?
It never happened. I grew up,
became a teen mother, pretending to be a poet.

In 2009 my friend, Margo — a bird, a real writer, a wise one,
took me to Shakespeare and Company, on the Left Bank.
She was well published in real University Press books.
Margo was first-name-friends with George Whitman,
proprietor of the legendary tumbleweed house of
moldy books and bright Paris memories.

Margo Bird whispered, we must not disturb George.
I could smell he was upstairs and now 96 years old,
and I really wanted to disturb him.

Sylvia, his daughter, came to us as we shopped
for bargains on the sidewalk,
"Come up, he's calling you."
I held back, thinking it was only for Margo Bird to fly up those stairs.
Sylvia swept me onward, with her eyebrows.

I had to gasp.
At the big round table sat two old men,
decrepit bowls of half-eaten food, and stacks of books.
I saw my own handmade poetry books tossed up there,
on the altar of Dharma Bums, like leaves fallen
so close to the knotted arthritic hands of Lawrence Ferlinghetti.

Was this real? Or had these ancients crawled
out of the rag and bone shop of my romantic heart?
Would Yeats resurrect and come strolling out of the bathroom,
tucking in his shirt?
Was George making places for us to sit,
fixing to serve up Neruda too?

Honestly, I don't know what was said.
When it was time to climb down the ladder,
cross the Seine, back to Margo's dark red wine abode,
I had agreed to make lunch for Whitman and Ferlinghetti.
Because I am Filipina, and they desperately wished
to eat Chicken Adobo.

Oh, the fowl that died and ginger knots uprooted for our feast.
There were no clean dishes.

# Daughter of a Cracked Dragon Teacup from Chinatown

There were rhinoceros penises and teapots
for sale on Jackson Street
near the Fortune Cookie factory.
We ate *Baozi* and *Jiaozi*, the little ear dumplings,
with laughter sauce.
Steam rose to dance a moment
with the Golden Gate to America fog,
where fire-breathing reptile trucks exhale exhaust fumes
that become big cloud dreams along the unkind bay.

San Francisco … My daughter learned her Asian heritage
in your cement and sidewalk flower cracked dragon district.
Pregnant with her, I fought a cop,
for my right to park. He wanted my space
for "Official Business."
Official business! This is just your lunch break?
Go find your own parking place! We all gotta eat.

Daughter Zhòu studied and became a doctor
of Traditional Chinese Medicine in your venerated city
of PhDs and trash bins. Filipina Lola wanted
her to be a medical doctor, like on television.
Plenty stink eye was cast around that Year of the Wood Horse.

I visited Zhòu's room, walls full of yellow Post-it paper
in neat rows. Each displayed a Chinese character,
the Ancestors' way of writing the meanings of medicines.
I learned my black-eyed child had become a healer.

She pushed a needle,
then a dozen into my hurt knee.

I grew so proud that the knives in my heart
from being beat up as a small kid because "Your mama's a nigger!"
flew back to hell. Even my scars softened.
I anticipated earth tremors.
She added needles in my kidney and gall bladder points.
I smelled sea fish and egg porridge, sour fire smoke
fueled by the overheat of Earth, and Santa Ana winds, too near.

Global Pandemic arrived quietly, like a Metal Rat,
they say, from China.
Don't go in the street, daughter!
White men blame us.
If they spit on you, I die.
That cop I fought, he called me, "Fucking Dragon Lady."
I was, I am, prideful.  I don't suffer insults anymore.

# Words Take Wing

After *Language of the Birds*, a San Francisco streetscape installation
by Brian Goggin and Dorka Keehnin at Broadway and Columbus

After sixty-some years of being cooped up
The books take flight like pigeons
from Ferlinghetti's City Lights Bookstore
Shapeshifted into polycarbonate, their opened pages
and bindings into wings as they fly
empowered by sun and wind

They stay a stone's throw
from the only home they've ever known
Fly in circles high above tourist talk, horn honk
homeless pleas and street musicians

Their guano drops as words
that recycle local literature and culture
That plant themselves into the plaza pavement
separating Chinatown and North Beach
Phrases as multilingual as the English, Italian
and Chinese that surrounds them

These bird/books never rest
Both day and night they illuminate
their readers with the Sun God's celestial power
In their reach for greater readership
they choose this affirmation of tolerance
and integration over the Pacific Ocean's siren song
crooking its finger of instinct

---

The "language of the birds" has a long history in mythology,
medieval literature and occultism as a mystical, divine language
used by birds to communicate with those initiated.

# Edge of Night

Black with blue swollen veins
He sits in stained denim
on the train station bench

Elbows on spread-eagled knees
Sparrow hands on head hung low
A plastic produce bag for a hat

pulled over his ears
Preserving the rising heat
The fragile lobes from frostbite

As winter eats its way
into the San Francisco Bay
with butcher knife teeth

# Fog

We don't have snow here
but some mornings the whole world
is white and hushed and soft with fog
and whatever troubles we went to sleep
clutched to our thudding hearts
have loosened overnight and are dissolving
in mist. The regal hills
to the East have been erased
behind a cottony scrim, and people
appear to appear
out of nowhere in the dawn hush.
An old woman in mask and gloves
pushes her shopping cart
full of salvaged empties. A mother hauls
two babies up the street, one in a backpack,
one in a stroller. A man
with dreadlocks and headphones
cruises by on his bike,
no-hands. All of them
whoosh into the frame
and then vanish. Like the future, or the past,
or some other dimension, alive,
but invisible to us.

# Making My Way Down Market Street

Anyone wearing a dirty old down coat on a summer day
Or three dirty down coats, one over another
Or accompanied by a dog with a bandana around its neck
Anyone digging in a trash can,
like that old woman on Market Street,
Who hobbled off clutching her find,
a McDonald's bag, to her chest
Anyone hobbling
Anyone sleeping in a doorway, using a duffel bag or an old pizza
box for a pillow
Like that young man who resembled my friend
the unemployed actor Thinning fog shrouds Sutro Tower
same tousled brown hair and long limbs, alert, slender face
For a moment I was startled thinking No, it couldn't be him
He has a mother who loves him, friends —
he's going on auditions . . .
But of course it wasn't him, it was another him
Anyone whose hair is wild, unkempt, gray-streaked, beastly
Although that could also be me, mornings when I haven't applied
Leave-in conditioner plus hair gel plus a little makeup
And instead walk into the world as my animal self,
All snarls and smells and curlicues,
Wild thoughts and just some used-to-be-middle-class manners
Thrown hastily on top of the whole catastrophe
My God, I think, making hard for the train,
Jaw clenched, ticket gripped in my fist,
Not turning to look around, not giving quarter to anyone —
Behold the slender threads
On which we are all hanging

# Haight and Ashbury

Not far from where my sister lived during
the sixties, I enter a three-story house where a family lives now.

My client is waiting and she shows me around
where the ghosts have been haunting her family.

I feel them around us, teasing then hiding from room to room.
I start in the kitchen and move through two floors with her
behind me.

*My daughter is psychic too*, she says, *will you talk with her?*
Her mother introduces us. The girl tells me they come to her at
night.

She brings me to her room in the attic.
I clear it and the closet that wraps around her room.

*They've been using this like a tunnel to escape.* I say.
*They just want attention, and can tell you see them.*

I say to her, *You have to manage your fear.*
*They just want a way through to the other side.*  Like this.

We chase them into the light.

*The trick is to ground yourself first. But don't take this on*
*if you are not up to it. You are only fifteen. You have lots of time.*

She smiles, and shows me the view. Below I can see where
my sister and her baby were robbed in their dingy flat. I wonder

if the ghosts in this home were the same ones
who were then on acid with guns.

*Wow,* I say to the girl, *you can see all the way to the park!*
*And the hospital on the hill!* she adds. *I want to be a doctor.*

*You will be a great doctor, we need psychic doctors!*
I give her more clues, and my time is up.

Downstairs the woman waits for us. She whispers. *My husband*
*came home, he is a computer whiz, and doesn't get this. But I do.*

I smile and greet him. She pays me and I hug both
the woman and her daughter. On my way out, I turn to the girl,

*Remember what I told you. Ground first, and*
*don't take this on if you are not up to it.* She grins and nods.

I walk out grateful and glad that I have passed
on some sort of torch to another seer.

## Contiguous

Don't you wonder about the panhandler
on Fremont and Market, sharing the day's
proceeds with his pink-nosed pit? Or

Frank Chu, with his sign of 12 Galaxies?
What about the World-Famous Bushman,
hiding behind the branch he shakes

at passers-by, or the matching — from pumps
to pillbox hats — Marian and Vivian Brown.
Who are they and who are you, staring out

from the glass eyes of your flat? Do you
awake in a sweat on an October night
with stars, the moon a fat orange

and the temperature pushing ninety
and remember a silver ring buried
under the azalea, the mute orphan who lived

with his uncle, your father who gave you
the back of his hand? Do you, like Frank,
dream of aliens? I'll bet the man on Fremont

dreams of Thunderbird and wakes up
as if he drank a whole bottle of fortified wine.
Nights like this, with windows wide, you can

hear the rush of the freeway, like the sound
of whitewater Ronald Reagan had piped
into his bedroom for insomnia. Nights like this

we lie naked, contiguous in this warm
ocean that flows around our backs and breasts
our arms our throats our lips, necks, thighs.

# Why We Have Windows

## 1. Home

Pinkest of parkas, darkest of
shades, the woman pushing the cart
down the sloped curb of my neighbor's
driveway veils her face, preserves a
privacy as she ferries bag
after bag bursting with cans, thinned
perhaps, by a stomp of her foot,
a quick, bold act punctuating
this winter day in our city,
hers and mine. I can study her
sneakers from here, note their newness,
imagine the sound — shoe sculpting
aluminum. The crack of a
pistol? Whip interrogating
skin? No. This woman, an elder
of our tribe, may bless, thank, each can,
change its shape, send it on its way.

## 2. Market

Yes, it is vanity that keeps
me here, unfolding frame after
frame of designer eyewear, six
floors up. "Hey! Somebody famous
down there!" A fellow myopic
shopper, delighted, drums on the
thick pane separating us from
winter in the city. I gape,
no, squint, with her at the passing
motorcade, each of us gifted
with temporary spectacles,
imagination, glee. X-ray

vision! "I bet it's the Irish
President," I say. "They move them
around," she says, "they never ride
in the same car." "I bet she's in
that one." I point at the limo
most veiled, most shaded, and we fall
silent, considering the stopped
traffic, the whistling of police,
the ways we keep each other safe.

## 3. Temple

This day after the rain may be
the best for walking Stow Lake. Few
others are here — a jogger, three
Russian ladies bundled and scarved
from the Avenues, clear plastic
galoshes snapped over their shoes.
I may be looking for something.
Yes, blue herons. Yes, turtles on
thin logs.  What breathes beneath the veils
our tribe creates.  I find comfort
here, solace in hushed benches
slippery now, their small, wet plaques
honoring past seekers, donors.
And nearing the boathouse, I glimpse
one employee, a teen, unrushed,
no snack bar orders to fill, no
canoes to rent. She stands at a
window, looking out, not at the
lake.  She faces another way,
perhaps her future.  She looks at
a sprinkling of cars parked in the
lot, beginning slowly to dry.

# Renter Sonnet #3

I say a prayer for cats dotting windows
and huddling under cars, spooked by this street,
the plump who snooze serene in rooms, and those
whose faces, sizes, names, quirks, and complete
health charts cram flyers tacked to poles.
Rewards are promised, coaxing safe return
of Spanky, Ringo, Cinnamon, Marbles,
asthmatic, microchipped, and shy. Who earns
these prizes? Anyone? Hope withers, wanes
in each apartment on this block. The time
we mourn does vary; some may entertain
their guests of grief for years, no new pets. I'm
inclined to wait, gaze through this glass, revere
the wordless, wild or tame, missing or here.

# Fog

[Morning]

The raven-haired beauty with apricot hips
sits with her coffee, reads.
It's a false cool day.
There's a fog coming in.
In the café the cook fries bacon,
roasts beans, builds heat —
and Ravenhair gets up to go.
I wish she would not: I like her curls,
like a murder of crows. But she flies away,
down the boulevard,
against the thickening sky.

[Fog]

I would like to view it under a microscope,
smoosh the sputtering droplets
between glass.
*Fog is only different from mist,*
reads the encyclopedia,
*for its density.* Thick sheets close off Marin,
hide the East Bay,
obscure the Presidio.
Above which:
a bushy canopy of green,
and somewhere a road,
and a gray grove of eucalyptus.

[Noon]

I wonder where it lives? Horn
moans low over stones and sea.

Oh and there are two —
listen closely — one resplendent,
one faint,
like port and starboard
or a near-and-far galaxy.
I want the distant one
to wrap its long voice across the waves,
cross this ocean,
and sing me to sleep.

[Lust]

The man in the coffee shop, newly awake, says:
*I wonder what it would be like*
*to live above something.* The law, I think,
or dew point. But he means a store or a deli.
I think treeline and weather balloon,
Hades, and the pinnacle
where lightning begins to crack.
Perhaps he means Ravenhair,
hips anchored
beneath him, a thousand crows
fanning out over his pillow.

[Dusk]

Crows collide. The lighthouse is shrouded, the man in there
flinching from ships. Even the gulls have stopped wheeling; the
seas are too high. Night, oh night. And oh morning.

[Fog]

*I want to have a good day,*
thought Ravenhair, disappearing
into the curtain on Clement Street.

*I want to have a good day,*
thought the man, wondering
how she would look in his bed.

*I want to have a good day,*
prayed the lighthouse attendant
as night became morning

and through a break in the curtain
he saw land,
sea,

and a ship passing through.
I have a voice after all.
I will sing to you from my tower.

# Things to Be Grateful for in San Francisco

White-crowned sparrows,
flowering trees,
firecracker paper,
lion dancers,
railroad flats,
bay windows,
pocket doors,
Lincrusta Walton,
bougainvillea,
stairway streets,
tiled storefronts,
witch-capped towers,
electric buses,
old streetcars,
cable car bells,
rollercoaster hills,
little houses inside city blocks,
wild parrots,
stratus clouds,
salt air,
low blue fog,
sourdough,
espresso,
sidewalk tables,
Dungeness crab,
pho, focaccia,
bulgoki, gnocchi,
moonrise over North Beach,
moonlight on the bay.

# Riding the 30 Stockton

Outside the bus the world sinks deeper:
So far two days and a night of solid rain,
and tonight the streets fill with dark paint;
the houses and buildings groan
like swimmers reluctant to enter the sea.
The windows of the bus run black
and silver. In the white fluorescent light
each damp face in the rows of faces is fleshy,
thickened. Inside my grocery bag a loaf
of sweet French bread is sending up
such small fat clouds of scent
I close my eyes with joy.

# Sunset on the 38 Geary

Each face staring straight ahead, no one speaking,
each rider holding the day carefully, like an egg,
past the piroshki bakeries, past the restaurants
selling *pho* and *bulgoki* and Shanghai dumplings
and *carnitas*, past the Church of the Star of the Sea
on the long blocks of the Outer Lands,
cement-covered sand dunes reaching out
to the Pacific and the blinding sunset light.
When the bus stops to let the people embark and
disembark, it makes a sound like baby wolves
howling at the moon. We drive on west, into
the sun. Each time the back door opens
it makes a sound like waterfowl
lifting from a lake. And we are hopeful,
even the old ones who struggle up the steps
to slowly ease into the seats reserved for them
and for the injured, and the young ones who think
they never will be old, for we believe that we will be delivered,
that we will be transported in our earthly bodies,
traveling as we are toward Avalon, the Island of the Blest,
with its golden apples and its lake of fire.

# Carnaval in San Francisco

*Carnaval* — a dream of sun
and the Mission District is rocking
with mariachi music, calypso, and reggae.
Muscular women gyrate in high-heeled gold boots,
*samba* into San Francisco's foggy heart.
Crowned with headdresses
hot-glued with rhinestones, beads, cowrie shells,
their hip circles mesmerize.
Gods and goddesses *bachata*
from Brazil, Panama, Trinidad;
kings and queens shimmy on floats of flowers.
Our gray city is transformed
into a rainbow of sequins and feathers.

Women drummers pound *tamboras, congas,*
shake cowbells at the sky.
The fierce rhythm reverberates in hundreds of hearts.
Black and brown, round and skinny,
*abuelas* sway with their grandchildren,
feet flying, smiles bright as hope.
Aztec dancers in eagle feathers
rattle *concha* shells, moving in prayer.
We follow the low-riders,
their growling hydraulics.
Cherry-red and metallic-blue,
these cars are intricate shrines,
tattooed with visions.

Stilt walkers in flowing gold and silver
lead children dressed as unicorns,
luna moths, monarch butterflies.
Spectators leap to grab teal and purple beads.

We channel *Oya*,
call on her warrior spirit,
move with earth's fire.
Our turns precise, our lines tight,
our skirts prayer flags
of bright orange, hot pink, and turquoise.
We dance for freedom, for justice,
sing for the voiceless.
We dance to honor our ancestors'
roots of resistance, their immigrant strength.
Our grandmothers shower blessings
from the hovering clouds.

# Ode to Alemany Farmers Market, 2020

Our Farmers Market is still a sanctuary
of Spring plenty: blueberries, early peaches.
Juan sings of white tulips.
Rosie sells bachelor buttons bluer than my mother's eyes.
I want to paint the creamy casaba melons,
the broccoli piled in heaping mounds,
the oceans of kale and chard.
We still rise early for our favorite Saturday ritual,
but now we hide behind masks and gloves,
wait in Russian bread lines.
We zig away from those who zag too close,
until we realize they're old friends.
We forage for the crispest spinach
the most fragrant basil for pesto and sauces.
The farmers choose our produce now.
No touching with bare hands.
We learn to smile with our eyes.
We bow in thanks.

## Ode to Lucca Ravioli

My kids grew up at Lucca Ravioli,
that quintessential deli in San Francisco's Mission.
Beautiful Italian men tended to them carefully.

They toddled there on fat legs, hair all blowy,
sat on counters, drooled at stunning food compositions.
My kids grew up, full, at Lucca Ravioli.

So many dinners of pasta and sauce for our family;
pancetta, prosciutto, parmigiano.
Beautiful Italian men fed us all, so carefully.

94 years on the same corner. The place is almost holy.
No useless shops then, no tech bros making acquisitions.
My kids grew up, innocent, at Lucca Ravioli.

94 years – over and gone. That holy ground will be wholly
disturbed. Overpriced condos? $12 juices? SF's new religion.
Those beautiful Italian men left us bereft — carefully sent packing.

Lucca's closed today. It filled slowly
with distraught locals — no one had asked our permission.
My kids grew up, loving and happy, at Lucca Ravioli.
Beautiful Italian men tended to them so carefully.

# The Case of the Six-Sided Dream

Downstairs they're cooking rice
to go with something that used to run off-leash
and trilling along with the TV.

Through the far wall, our landlord is dying in his sleep,
a little each night.

In the front yard he tore the last tree from the block.

Out back he wills his drought upon the blackened hedge.

Our southern neighbors are hammering nails again.
There's more metal than wood in their walls
and a picture hung
for every day since Creation.          In an unaccountable

caesura of neighborly silence

rain sweeps the roof
riprapping a Roland Kirk rag, like
when the drummer comes brushing in,
and you know the reeds are right behind,
calling all dimensions to a collision
in tune.

# A Partial Bestiary for Burning Libraries

I think of burning libraries,
Alexandria for one.

I think of the Taliban looking to burn every scroll
in Bamako that might reveal Islam's
thirst for inquiry.
I think of the real radicals, librarians
secreting truths downriver:

Constellations of gazelle skin and papyrus.
Ink etched on chary genealogies
older than the astronomer's proofs, but not what he's proven,
and generations of scholarship
visiting and revisiting his transit of Venus in the margins;
a distance of suns running nocturnal rapids
out of Timbuktu.

I think of the librarian who lives
over his corner store. He sighs in smoke over Carthage, still,
and Jaffna more recently,
bemoaning bachelorhood and a dusty degree in Classics
before extinguishing the neon and ascending to his desk
to tap-tap away the overdue hours.

He remembers aloud, lips moving in Oxford-accented Tamil,
until I approach the counter.

"*There is a name for every known species*
*glossed in the slippage of a dead language*
*for a living science,*" he says.

There is talk of a palm leaf library back in Sri Lanka,
chloroplasts imprinted with the Buddha's words,

harvesters of light,
sutras burning in protest of impermanence,
if I have my politics correct.

Some nights I hear his typewriter keys clacking
from down on the sidewalk
while out for my insomniac stroll.
I look into his eyes and down at the cold silver in my palm,
do the math on jungle fires.

*"Do you think there is a poem for every species?*
*One unaware of the other, mostly,*
*a dying ratio of dying concern?"* he asks.

Now I know he's seen me out walking.
It brings to mind larger questions
of balance.

Our neighborhood was teetering on the brink of extinction
until the liquor store opened its doors.

*"Water to wine is just a parlor trick,"* he says,
*but it always draws a crowd*
*so here I am."*

*"You must know,"* he adds, surveying his magazine rack,
*"words are all we have*
*for assembling granite from ash."*

Sitting before the rows and rows
of bottles, redolent with his Tiparillos,
he doesn't touch a drop.
This is his potshot at martyrdom, this
counting out change
while drawerfuls, reams of

Olivetti-sparked words, ignite his upstairs apartment:
a library of the mind burning down present tense San Francisco,
burning in disbelief, he believes
for nobody else.

# I Read Virgil

After a sleepless night, I read Virgil,
cradling first light in my hands.

Pages resound. Ancient words rise —
freedom exists beyond Troy's broken walls.

I stand beside my bookshelf at the window
looking at the morning streets.

I raise my hand to the garbage man
making his Thursday rounds, a man who has it all.

He nods and goes on his way,
loaded down with future archeology.

Weather rages. Power lines rattle the air.

Jealous gods hurl their elements
at us mortals and the moaning jaws of the garbage truck.

Every line held, it seemed, so that

voices once without a book
ferried in biremes might
cross time's doldrums
and find another city
in these ever-dying hands.

# The Mist is Settling on Everything

The mist is settling on everything.
The train splashes past. The house rumbles in its wake.
The heat clicks on in the middle of spring.
I close all the windows.

Way across San Francisco the sun is blazing.
Everyone is sure of it.
Out here by the ocean the land simply draws more water.
The sky is weighted, low slung, not bothering to fall, what
with water rising to meet it.

Out here, our street is like the others:
Alphabetical, neatly numbered in a nautical grid,
now submerged beside the park
where the oldest trees sway like rooted water lilies
buoyed in the sky.

Ornithologists consult swell maps and crane their necks
up to canopies where
birds flit like water bugs
skating the even stratospheres.
It is a rare migratory season, a day in length if that.

Already, the sun is settling on everything. Waters recede.
I open a second story window, just above the flood zone again,
drainpipes done with their music.
Seated upon the neighbor's olive branch
a crow thinks to caw
waiting for the ground to reappear
glistening black in remnants of thinning silent mist.

# 16th & Valencia

I saw Jack Micheline on the corner of 16th & Valencia
reciting "Skinny Dynamite" and he was angry
and the next day he was dead
on the last BART train to Concord
and maybe that's why he was angry
I met Harold Norse shuffling around in a beaten world
his pockets stuffed with poems only hipsters read
It's a cesspool out here he sighed
before retreating to his room in the Albion Hotel
where angels honeycomb the walls with dreams
and the rent is paid with angry poems
I heard Oscar Zeta Acosta's brown buffalo footsteps
pounding the Valencia Corridor
and he was shouting poetry at the sick junkies
nodding with their wasted whores
in the lobby of the Hotel Royan "The Mission's finest"
and even the furniture was angry
I joined the waiters at the bus stop
the waitresses the norteños trios the flowers sellers
the blind guitarist wailing boleros at a purple sky
the shirtless vagrant vagabond ranting at a parking meter
the spray paint visionary setting fire to the word
and I knew this was the last call
We were tired of living from the scraps of others
We were tired of dying for our own chunk of nothing
And I saw this barrio as a freight train
a crazy Mexican bus careening out of control
a mutiny aboard a battleship
and every porthole filled with anger
And we were going to stay angry
And we were not leaving
Not ever leaving
El corazón del corazón de La Misión
El Camino Real ends here

# Silicon City

They evicted Mia from her storefront on Valencia
Then they burned down the apartments on 22nd Street
The good die young and isn't it a pity
But the beat goes on in Silicon City

You're a stranger now in your home town
With strange faces on once familiar streets
And strange shadows at four o'clock
And cops strangers on a strange beat
The days and nights are mostly gritty
But hey, it's ok, you're hanging in Silicon City

So I've been told that everything that rises must fall
And that the wicked shall be denied
But nowadays you don't know who to trust
And watch out you don't get run over by a Google bus
It be's that way all down and dirty
In the heartless heart of Silicon City

Now everybody knows the center cannot hold
But prophecy is cheap and politicians are slippery
So baby get your high-heeled sneakers and your black beret on
Because tonight we fight the power in Silicon City

# Ode to a Golden Icon

You loom over choppy waters
summoning reverential fear
like a rust-colored Pterodactyl
with its wings spanning the foggy skyline —
an anthem of praise to the city,
taunting Alcatraz from a distance.

Bundled in mist
and a spring jacket,
grateful for the sloppy scarf
around my neck
as sea-breeze and high anxiety
seep into my pores,
we walk in the womb
of the early morning
across the Golden Gate Bridge.

Some have traveled by bus, car, and bicycle
to the allure of a gate where souls have perished.
How many sacrifices have you attained
to remain standing?
What dour soul,
solitary and doleful,
lies encased in your foundation?

# Where I Live

The one-armed white man
with dreadlocks
scouts the traffic below
the 101 underpass
for spare change.
His face is an abandoned building,
his body a burned-out battlefield.
His broken shoes slap the asphalt as he navigates
the fenders and rear-view mirrors.
*Even a smile will help*, his sign reads.
We roll up our windows.
The car ahead moves on and we rush
to step on the gas. Later, at home,
roses bloom in the window.
The table is set with silver.
The food is ready. We slice the bread.
Eat.

# Presidio

Haven of trees above the Gate,
windy, black-winged, wet,
harbored springs clean as Shasta's,
and if you wandered the ravines,
watercress found you too.

Between beatniks and empty barracks
Julius Kahn's monkey bars dazzled.
The little Jewish girl and I dizzied
down the daisy-dotted slopes
and draped our necks with pollen-dusted rope.

Away from ballerinas and babysitters
the dark cypress grove beckoned.
Beneath black branches, in dens of sand,
at home in the wild and make-believe,
we traded seeds and secrets.

## Magic from Chinatown

Daddy's treat in a plastic bag,
black-gray clam
smaller than a quarter
we submerged in the kitchen sink.

Hour by hour
the bi-valve soaked up water
then suddenly cracked open.
In another hour
a stem emerged
and over the next few hours
lengthened toward our faces.

Eventually
pink and yellow petals unfurled.

Every secret, stranger, lover, moon
a surprise
staggering up through watery depths
toward light,
prying itself open from within,
blossoming.

Flower Face, I call you,
Camellia Ears,
Rose Lips.

# Scars of Tempeh

Our towels were frayed and the dog was sleeping in the middle of this scuttled floor. I did my job: pizza ordered, no salad. The youngest cat yowling his baby sound, hairball imminent. The overlapping waves why we moved here, the sky and the Cliff House. And the feeling that this was fresh. Memories rise from the mind like lint. The day we drove by the Cliff House, so happy on the dumb curves. We didn't own one dish, but we had a wok and could fry scars of tempeh, enough to say we were alive. Just enough to want an orange sunset together, leaning.

# Rice Paper and Luck

In Chinatown they all look hungry. My once loving husband is visiting his doll, and I'm coasting down Russian Hill in my rusty old car, singing songs nobody remembers. Do you see me slumped in the back of Al Wing's Chinese restaurant, slurping congee with a man who wants me but hasn't got the equipment?

What are we doing here? I say.

He winks, sighs, fondles my knee.

To him, this date is made of rice paper and luck.

He has dumpling cheeks, calls me Dragon Doll, wiggles his chopsticks at my lips.

"Suck this, little bird," he says. I imagine his overcooked noodle.

So I leave us both on the verge of happiness at Al Wing's, our fortune cookies still intact. I'll call this photo "Christmas in Chinatown," fall asleep alone in my car, wrestle with the memory of my ex and me seeing Chinatown for the first time together. Christmas. How happy we were to know that world existed. Lining up at the tofu truck, holding fingers.

# Marina Safeway, San Francisco

*for Armistead Maupin*

*March 25, 2019*

Pigeons congregate in an empty parking space,
spilling over the lines. I stand for a moment as
seagulls upset the still with their flight and cry,
swirl the air gray. Then I go in, and no, not to
Whitman, not to Lorca, or even Allen Ginsberg.
I hope to find Michael Tolliver traipsing through
the aisles with Mary Ann Singleton — any of them —
the Barbary Lane beloveds. Still naive and new.

Yesterday, my 43rd birthday, Lawrence Ferlinghetti's
100th. Everyone mobbed Columbus Avenue, City Lights,
like those parking lot pigeons, spilling over the lines,
listening to poetry, words that fed a great generation.
The Beats. I'm sentimental about eras I didn't live in.

In Marina Safeway, back in the day, before tech
millionaires, before the impending influx of more,
before mylar balloons now on display that choke
our birds, our Bay, before San Francisco changed over,
I'd have roller-skated my way between high pyramids
of avocados and bananas — myself high — not waiting
for their ripeness, not asking their cost, or mine.
Woken up blissful with anyone, not fearing death.

That Angel had not yet arrived here, unrolling a river,
merciless and vast, on which you saw all your friends
float by: wasted to bones, so young and afraid, dying
one after another. Beautiful, then gone. Just gone.
Whitman, Lorca, these are your dead, your children.

Do not turn from them. The Bay is wider than a river.
Is that optimism or sorrow, America lost even then?
As we look forward, look back, was San Francisco?

# Sitting Above the Orchestra

*Dedicated, with gratitude,
to the musicians of the San Francisco Symphony*

Sitting above the players, born aloft
by the music: a hawk soaring above
a warm-toned sepia forest of stringed
instruments that may have sung together
long before they were caressed by these hands
that guide the bows and dance on the finger-
boards. Fingers of the left hand pressing strings
and shaking like the wind that once shook the
autumn leaves of the maple trees cut down
to make the backs and sides of the basses
and cellos, violas and violins.

The wind that first coaxed music from the trees
long before a luthier traced the grain of
Nature's song with plane and saw, rubbed as if
at a magic lamp with sand and oiled
rags. Varnished to a brilliance tight enough
to hold the highest notes that wrap around
the heart and squeeze. Lowest tones that echo
the pleasure-laden moaning of the breeze.

The tops of those instruments, the best ones,
made from spruce that grow in far northern lands,
ever green until they die — trees that live
for many centuries, then live again,
held with skillful hands against that secret
place between neck and chin that's also sought
by babies — a place where, on violists
and violinists, the skin is calloused
and scarred from a lifetime of practicing.
Marked like the bark of a tree that has rubbed
against another for years in the wind.

Who ever thought of going to Brazil
to harvest *pernambuco* for the bows?
Who lit on horses' tails to hair those bows
that, rosined, stroke the strings with just the right
amount of sticking and sliding to make
the music soar like a hawk, higher and
higher, till the last sweet notes disappear?

It's clear, looking at the men and women
clothed in black and white and tails, their faces
marked by life, and some of them with hair gone
white, that they themselves are well along on
the path to becoming trees. Growing leaves,
holding snow and giving back to the wind
the gift of their virtuosity. Their
instruments to be held and loved and coaxed
by younger hands to make music again.

Looking down, the hawk sees only forest —
past and future trees — as it's born aloft
by the sound. Sees the musicians as one
with the instruments they play, for whom they've
honed a lover's skill to fill the concert
hall with music written by composers
possessed by inspiration: breathing in
and writing down eternal notes gathered
in the dangerous dark where truth is found.

# Things I Would Show My Relatives If They Ever Came to Visit Me

First, I would take them
to see my friends.
My friend Susan
and her psychiatrist husband
in their Telegraph Hill apartment
with a view of the entire bay.

My friend Judy
living in a pre-earthquake building
on Bush Street —
*so* San Francisco
with a posted warning in the lobby
not to let strangers in
as two of the residents
have stalkers.

They could see my office,
now on a floor with a window
and they could meet my co-workers
who all like me.

We could have drinks
at the Fairmont,
where they know me
as I live right down the street.

And after all this
they would realize I'm normal after all.

# Mission Street Station

Running for the screeching sliding trains
in the underground station,
we all pass the street musicians.
In this year's windy wet winter
in the Mission,
where *mariachis* pop in and out
of Mission Street restaurants at night,
collecting their tips,
where *mariachis* usually stride
in threes and fours,
one lone *mariachi* and his guitar has taken up
the underground's little isle for musicians,
a *sombrero* on his head,
dressed in black,
like a lost bird
from the rest of
his *mariachi* flock.
He has become driven indoors
by the weather into a station
looking more stoic and solitary
than other street singers
without a concertina, an accordion,
and a big-bellied Spanish bass guitar,
or looking like a man escaped from a painting,
framed by his hat,
playing for coins.
His guitar echoes
through the countless people
returning from work,
in the high-arched cavern,
his notes merging with
the train's long caterwauling screeches,

as his fingers singe the strings
like lively dance steps
emigrated into this grotto,
one sound or another
claiming all their souls.

# Cold

At a bus stop,
On a cold day
In San Francisco.
In Union Square,
Grannies sing
Against war;
A woman at a Mission bus stop
Asks where she can
Buy a blanket,
I don't usually shop at big stores,
She wants one nice
But not costly,
I point to Cliff's Five and Dime,
We do what we
Can to keep warm.

# Windows

Peter balances on the ladder,
to wash the City Lights Bookstore's windows.
It is a regular job.
One must think
that Ferlinghetti
values very clean windows;
books on ledges peering out,
customers' noses peering in.
In this work,
there is nothing mechanical
about finding the elegant curves
of the glass and moldings.
I remember my mother
having a window washer
occasionally clean
the windows in our
old house.
In my new address,
almost a railroad flat,
there are hardly any
windows.
Windows are like eyes,
and eyes are where
the soul resides
and City Lights has
the cleanest windows
in town.

# Bookends

I'd just jotted down an idea for a poem when the two pit bulls bolted from the bushes. One positioned its snout against my rear and the other deep into my groin. They looked like small sharks with feet. I stopped, forgetting how to breathe.

I was in a park I'd often driven past but had never been to before. It seemed a good place for a walk.

"Who you with?" a voice said.

When I turned to look, the dogs dug in deeper, snarling.

"Don't move, asshole, less you wanna go from a *he* to a *she*."

"Whoa..."

"I'll ask you again—who you with?"

"Just me," I said.

"You a wise-ass?"

"Sorry," I told him, without knowing what I was apologizing for. He stepped in front of me, a full head shorter with a nasty twist to his mouth, his head tilted to one side. He wore a red hoodie and pointed to my chest. His pits seemed content enough bookending the slim volume I'd become.

"Your colors," he said, "you're sporting your colors."

"This?" I followed his eyes, pointed to the top of my running suit.

"Don't play with me, man."

Confusion merged with panic. It was an awful mix. "This shirt?" I asked, tugging at the material.

"Thems CLD colors," he said. "Don't play dumb, sucker."

"You mean like a gang? I'm not in a gang. I'm a poet," I told him.

"Faggot," he said.

My running suit was getting saliva-basted and I simultaneously anticipated unbearable pain and sudden loss.

"You don't wear blue in this park," he said. He did some kind of hand gestures, curling his wrists and forming his fingers into a distinct pattern and shot them in front of my face.

"But it's not blue," I told him.

"That's blue," he insisted.

"Actually it's kind of green. But I can see how it might *look* blue in this light."

He had a thin V-shaped goatee which he scratched with one finger.

I was hoping his dogs wouldn't attempt anything impromptu. He reached in his back pocket and removed a narrow paint chip book and fanned it out. "You gonna be missing some parts if you bullshitting me."

"Green," I repeated with a little voice.

He held a panel of graduated hues against my running top.

"You mind if I look?" I asked, peering down. He grunted.

"Sassy Grass," I said. "Well, sort of between Sassy Grass and Kryptonite Green."

"Humm," he said, holding the sample against my chest. "You just mighta hit the jackpot, sucker." He twisted his fingers up into that configuration again, which seemed to mean so much to him, flashing it in front of my eyes. Then he said something in a foreign language or a slang I couldn't understand, and the dogs relented — flanked him as he walked back through the bushes.

I stood there for a moment with the sun on me, as though I were defrosting, with the word *Kryptonite* knocking around in my head, thinking: Go figure, some fake element from an imaginary world just saved me.

# Measuring the Distance

My sister visits — her head ablaze with new drama. Her history is stunning. She has escaped the Moonies, a voodoo cult, survived a biker who chained her to the bed. And after each grand opera when, amazed, she finds the stage sets collapsed upon her, she visits.

Now, it's a defrocked priest who's left her. "I snipped the tips off all his rubbers," she says, as we're walking through the park a few blocks from my house. "I figured, why be subtle, right? I'm not getting any younger. I want to experience motherhood at least once before I kick."

I listen. I nod. It's what I do. I could be a parking meter or a can of peaches, it wouldn't matter. When we turn toward the baseball diamonds in Golden Gate Park, I hear the *beeping*. See the blind players on the field, their heads tilted, listening for the *beep … beep … beep …*

I've seen this once before. A game of "beep-ball" played in the dark on a sunny day. And steer us toward it. We sit on a slope above the field and she doesn't miss a beat.

"And the son of a bitch took Sparky. You remember Sparky? That stray we took in. I told you about him over the phone."

"Sure," I say, but my head is in the game. A sighted pitcher slow-tosses the beeping ball to a blind batter. The batter listens, poised for that perfect moment when the sound is loudest. He swings, connects; a miracle of timing — a ground ball off the tip of the bat. It slow-rolls on the grass. The blind fielders, gauging its coordinates, tap the ground closing in; pushing through an erased world tarred black. Occasionally, I nod, say, "Wow," "Hmm," as my sister chatters on.

There are guide dogs on the sidelines, patient in their harnesses —
friends and family cheering as the ball is located, held up to the
light. *The light.* I pull my cap down, shut my eyes. Hear: "Shit
head" ... "Religious hang ups" ... "Lousy lay" ...

I imagine the sound of it, that *beeping* coming closer, in the dark;
that black molasses to push through or drown in. Could I meet
it, chest out, and connect as gloriously as they?

When I open my eyes again, everything is brighter, clearer. There's
a wedge of sunlight on my sister's dress, highlighting a single rose.

"Look," I say, pointing. "The way the light ..."

"The light — what light?  You're not listening to a thing I'm
saying," she accuses, then glances around as though suddenly
snapped out of a trance. "And what's that God-awful beeping?"
she says. "Huh?  Can you answer me that?"

## After the Earthquake

During the blackout we listen to news on my daughter's clown radio, tuning in disaster with a twist of a bulbous red nose.

Fearful the food will rot; we empty out the fridge and take it to the lawn, which night has erased. *Picnic*, my daughter says, giddy with play and innocence — the house of straw we exit, the big bad wolf could blow away at any moment.

Back inside, our child asleep on my lap. The clown radio on hers, empty now of news and spark. My wife asks if I'm still hungry. I shake my head. But it's dark. *What?* she says. *I'm good*, I tell her. Lighting another candle for the night to eat.

# Ode to the L Owl

4:46 am at Portola & Clipper
I catch you flying inbound.
You're a wise owl
and as your faithful student I heed

to the everyday,
the always, occasionally,
once-but-never-again rhythms
of the nocturnal commute.

To the long gray beard,
black leather jacket, and sunglasses
sitting perfectly still,
the composure of a monk.

To the terrier toting
a brown paper bag in her teeth
boarding at Castro
with her human sidekick.

To the drag queen's generous presence
beside the teenagers at Church Street, looping,
slumping slowly in their seats until they nearly fall
shaking themselves alert.

To the neatly dressed Chinese man at Van Ness
black jacket and pants
sitting down to reveal playful socks
sushi one day, hamburgers the next.

To the friends who greet each other at 9th Street
with a kiss on each cheek

in company of, only by proximity to,
the tourists lost after a night out.

To the exasperated woman
with the serrated knife in hand
who bursts in at 5th Street/Powell
rushing off at 4th Street/Stockton.

To the woman in the Subway polo
catching sleep until
her internal alarm clock
wakes her at 3rd Street/Kearny.

At 2nd Street/Montgomery I leave your steady eye
to study intricate choreography on sidewalks,
crosswalks, and staircases, until its
familiarity becomes epiphany becomes the lesson.

To read volumes pasted in chapters
on buildings, glowing from windows,
painted on the asphalt. To listen to
improvised lectures in retrospect.

Tomorrow I'll begin again,
progressing through the
syllabus illuminated by
headlights against the fog.

Maybe one day
I'll be absorbed into your curriculum and
pass whatever impossible test one must pass
to call this city home.

## Monterey Cypress

When young, how delicate
your tendrils, roots
undisturbed by rodents and rot.
Seedling scattered from bird's wing,
you gained a foothold.
Were there sister saplings
and fragrant shrubs?
Darkest green foliage,
like hair-fall, swayed
to strange enchantments.
Now alone. Roped off
so no one can carve initials,
deface shaggy bark.
In old age, your body
"haggard with storm-drift,"
bends inland, your trunk swivels —
    magnificent bonsai.
You turn away from grand frigates
and singing whales.
In the scent of drying kelp,
time to watch new lambs
in soft canyons, time
to welcome wintering Monarchs,
catch a sparrow's tail,
    feel the pale heart beating,
    then release.

# Tenderloin Darlings

Midnight.  She wheels
a baby carriage full of
bric-à-brac down the
Castro.  It contains
a bright red ukulele.

Dressed like a frog &
playing the clarinet
on Union Square ...

A local is lovely enough
to explain the scent and taste
of vegan excrement to me.

Nob Hill.  The building
manager lets me play
with her chameleon.
His name is Handbag.

Mother Goddess recites
Carl Sandburg in the back
of an Uber.  Her hair
has the texture of fog.

Blood or Kool-Aid?  Poop
or avocado?  The sidewalks
are always rife with mystery.

Huffing and puffing up California
Street arm in arm with a funky
septuagenarian named Carol.

There's something inherently
poetic about an old man eating
strawberries out of the trash.

A Rorschach-stained
écru Ultrasuede skirt
and cowboy boots: this
homeless drag queen
is absolutely killing it!

# Abandoned Bicycle

Behind her, a tree too young to climb,
a bicycle which jolts on roads

she does not wish to take.
Here in the Dante-dark wood pocked

with sun, she is freed from the spoke
and the spoken. Here the soft

scuff of Nike, crack of twig,
scumble of blackberry is everything.

No chain, no blacktop or bars.
Here only a basso of bullfrog

launched from a stagnant pond.
Her answer —

a quixotic pause, a nod,
a greedy silence.

## Street Cleaning Day

Jack looks like a normal guy. No one else is out
on the street, just him. He moves my car from Friday
to Monday, saving me from another ticket.

This is something he often does, two or three times
a week. I can see him in the fog, partly lit by street
lamps before blue morning glories open.

I watch him head out to work in his whites — that's
what they call a house painter's overalls. I can see
him, a beautiful phantom, with my eyes closed.

## Umbilical, 1983

I labored on the old yellow couch —
a shade of mustard I'll never
forget — and pushed until my face
flushed red with the blood we shared.

On the wall above my head, a painting
by Modigliani — a woman who resembled me
except for her eyes, which were closed
as if she slept, set apart from all
the bliss, the mess.

It was October — the sunniest
room of the house, where
back door opened onto apples,
and belly muscles turned inside out —
when your head finally crowned,
and you, my son, were stupendously born,
umbilical cord cut, yet not —
leaves churning, spinning beyond
the window, light playing at the edges
of spider lace curtains until it too
broke through to rapture.

# A Narrow Space

I park between
a little pyramid of clothes
hiking boots, her pale hand
tugging jacket buttons
and that young man almost in tears
because maybe
I put a scratch on his
hundred thousand dollar car.

# The History of Possibility

She sits in the café gazing
across the street at the Muni stop
and the newspaper racks and the tracks
shining in the morning sun, and she twirls
a strand of dark brown hair in her left hand
behind her head, twirls it through her fingers

as if weaving hair into daydream, counting time
with this resilient strand that seems
almost to be dancing with her hand,
or coiling like a snake or a ribbon around her fingers
then springing free and starting again.

This could go on for hours,
a little perpetual motion machine,
but suddenly she stops, stands up and walks a step
to meet the plain young man in the blue pea coat
strolling through the door. I want to say,
Don't waste this morning ordering eggs
and drinking orange juice. But she will, because

the casual beauty of the young, the light that shines
through the skin, the sheen in the hair,
is invisible to her now, eclipsed
by the desire to become someone more.
I feel like an angel standing at her shoulder,
whispering in her inattentive ear:
This is it. Nothing you do
will matter more than this.

## Camera Obscura

*A replica of Leonardo's invention, the Camera Obscura*
*is a dark room with a periscope that focuses an image*
*of the outside world on a white concave bowl. It sits*
*in San Francisco overlooking the Pacific Ocean.*

You don't start at the heart of it.
You start sightseeing, taking friends around
on a sunny afternoon. Stopping at the Cliff House,
you peer at the ruins of the gigantic pools
reduced to rubble like the foundations of Roman baths.
Passing the gift shops and trinket stands,

you walk down an ugly concrete stairway
to a viewing platform perched on a rocky outcropping
looking out at a steamer or two in the wide, impassive Pacific.
The Camera Obscura stands to one side, dressed up
like an old boxy camera, a sideshow at a penny arcade.
You pay your dollar to the ticket taker at the door

and feel your way inside into the funhouse darkness.
In the little circular room stands a shallow white bowl
the size of a table top, and in it floats
a world much like the one outside, but refracted
and sharpened to a soundless, immaculate image
of itself. You've just been admitted

to the antechamber of the angel entrusted
with gazing at the world and watching in wonder
as it dies each moment into a new birth.
The waves along the shore speak eloquently
of their rush to disappear into the sand.
You stand in the dark bumping into strangers
now and then as this device of Leonardo's
rotates through a complete circle, as if showing you

the earth meditating on its own detailed magnificence.
Like the earth seen from space, the bowl
is suspended in darkness; like the earth
in space, a canvas of light afloat in a void;
a canvas of light, remaking itself with each heartbeat;
each moment a new world becoming an old world becoming new.

# A Place Called Stoney Creek

Here in the city
people take care
of themselves
on the farm
(where you
grew up) every
thing takes care
of everything else.
cows take care of
horses, horses take
care of men, men
take care of barns &
plows & tractor engine
parts take care of each other.
bees take care of clover & clover
takes care of bees (who are also taken
care of by beekeepers) & the fields are
alive with California Poppies that wobble in
the orange-yellow breeze. I don't know
how these things work, I am just a man
of the city I'm lucky if I can take care of
myself one day to the next. But I try
best as I can & I leave the rest to
chance & dream that we don't
live here in the city at all, you &
me — we live up the coast in a
place called Stoney Creek,
Del Norte County, California,
we have milk goats & chickens
we have strong children, we teach
them right & we send them on their way
we have eggs & cheese butter & milk

we've got ducks in a duck pond, an old
fishing boat with a leak in the hull, &
in summer there's long grass for mowing
& in spring there's short grass for making love in,
under the yellow California sun (yellow
of marigolds, yellow of your hair) &
sometimes you admit it, you had a
boyfriend back in the day, a farm boy
(even now when you braid your hair
with wildflowers you sing songs
you learned from him) & I skin
my knuckles on spark plugs
& chromium steel & do not
mind & often in the morning
I stop to smile because you've
made some little present for
me, with your perfectly strong
hands, left it on the kitchen counter.
This is my dream, I do not wish
to ever be free of it in fact I had
it just the other night, my dream,
you & me we drove up the coast
to the Oregon border, we left SF
around midnight by the time we
hit Stoney Creek it was morning,
the fields were cool with Pacific fog —
& all the way there you sang songs
that farm boy taught you and all the
way there I fell in love with you, over
and over again — because that's what I
do in my dream about Stoney Creek.
I fall in love with you — like the first
love, like the first spring. Like any
ordinary old man from the city would
do. Because I know what love is. Love

is a field of tall yellow grass with orange-
yellow poppies waving their fool heads off
in the Pacific ocean breeze. Love is clover
for bees, bees for clover.

Love is a place called Stoney Creek — and you,
braiding those long strings of wildflowers in your golden hair.

# White-Haired Ladies on Monterey Blvd.

at yoga this morning,
      stretching into
           downward-dog,
                bottoms facing
                    fog-thick sky:
                        recalling times when,
                in patchouli-dark
            rooms in Victorian flats,
        Marvin Gaye
    on the tape-deck,
desire bloomed

admonished to
      *let the tailbone*
           *meet the pubic bone,*
                calves crossed
                    in half-lotus,
                        I ponder
                loss of pigment,
           as a hairdresser
        once discreetly
explained

and find
      a willowy joy
           in pressing
                toes against
                    thigh,
                        a tender
                balance
           in tree pose,
        awaiting word

of a first
grandchild

then imagine how
    later that night,
        the ponytailed
            assistant will
                wonder aloud
                    to her bemused
              boyfriend:
            do you think
        they still,
      you know,
*do it?*

# About the Poets

**Lynne Barnes** was born in Georgia and moved to New York City in 1968 with a front row ticket to HAIR, before migrating to San Francisco in 1969, two years after the Summer of Love. She was part of a commune that thrived for twenty years in the Haight Ashbury. She is a former psych nurse and librarian. Her poetry memoir, *Falling Into Flowers* (Blue Light Press), was the recipient of the 2017 Rainbow Award for Best Gay and Lesbian Poetry.

**Jeffrey S. Bartfeld** is a poet, image maker, and photographer of the cover of this book. For Jeffrey, poetry and image creation is an expression of soul. He seeks meaning in the space before him, often combining his images with poetry, as he hikes alone in forests and seashores or walks the streets of his favorite city, San Francisco, with camera, notebook and pencil in hand. He opens himself to the silence of his surroundings; listens to its whispers. In the cover image, the Golden Gate Strait, seething below its namesake bridge, bellowed its history to Jeffrey on a rainy San Francisco morning. He is author of *A Poet's Portrait of Point Reyes,* his debut collection of poems and photographs of Point Reyes National Seashore.

**Beau Beausoleil** has lived, worked, and written poetry in San Francisco for the last 50 years. He has always loved its people, neighborhoods, progressive politics, and even the enveloping fog. He has worked in and owned bookstores in the City for many years. He has lived with his wife, the artist Andrea Hassiba, in the Excelsior District for the last 25 years. As a non-driver, buses have always seemed to Beau like "moving democratic institutions" and he has taken them to and from work seemingly forever. His favorite bus routes are the #43 (when it enters the Presidio) and the #44 (as it rides along the edge of Glen Park Canyon). He is the author of 14 books of poetry and has always been proud to be referred to as a "San Francisco Poet."

**Marianne Betterly** — When she isn't writing poetry or videoing jaguars, Marianne Betterly travels the world photographing wings, windows and wanderers in various latitudes of light. She writes about synchronicity and spirits, flashbacks, and the streets of San Francisco. Her poetry has been published widely in books and journals including *River of Earth and Sky: Poems for the 21st Century, The Widows' Handbook, Between the Fault Lines, Turning a Train of Thought Upside Down, New Sun Rising: Stories for Japan, Hot Flashes, Green Silk Journal,* and the *Haight Ashbury Literary Journal.* Her book of poems, *The Return of the Bees,* was published in 2016 by Blue Light Press. Marianne lives in a house in Kensington overlooking San Francisco and the Golden Gate Bridge.

**Claudia Cole Bluhm** grew up in a working class San Francisco neighborhood. Her diary, Sarah, became her best friend. Life in the city filled her pages — fog racing over Twin Peaks each afternoon; dipping jelly doughnuts into milked-down coffee on Saturday mornings with her Gram and her brother; her father, nicknamed Harry the Horse, driving up in his T-bird convertible, a Camel cigarette perpetually hanging from his mouth. Her first book of poems, *At the End of my Walk,* was published by Blue Light Press in 2021.

**Abby Caplin** fell in love with San Francisco in the summer of 1964, at the age of nine, when she and her mother would take the bus down Market Street to buy carnations from the flower vendors at Union Square. They spent lots of time in Cost Plus, pretending to travel to different countries. San Francisco has been the place from which to launch her dreams of helping to make the world a better place. Her poems have appeared in *AGNI, Salt Hill, The Southampton Review, Tikkun,* and elsewhere. Among her other honors, she is a winner of the San Francisco Poets Eleven. She is a physician practicing mind-body medicine in San Francisco.

**Thomas Centolella** visited San Francisco on a balmy October day in 1977 and decided to stay. Since then he has become a Stegner Fellow at Stanford, published four books of poetry, and received a number of honors, including the Lannan Literary Award, a Guggenheim Fellowship, and the Northern California Book Award. When he isn't teaching at College of Marin or a private workshop, he can be found either on a golf course or in his aerie on top of a major San Francisco hill, ignoring the cable cars clanging by while working on a new poem, or on a song at his beloved Yamaha piano. His most recent book, *Almost Human*, is winner of the Dorset Prize from Tupelo Press.

**Dane Cervine** has lived in San Francisco whenever he can — Noe Valley, the Mission District — has attended graduate school, professional conferences, almost living in the museums, imbibing the arts, and haunting bookstores. Living now in Santa Cruz, he still crosses the border regularly, feeling right at home each time. His recent books include *Earth Is a Fickle Dancer* (Main Street Rag), and *The Gateless Gate — Polishing the Moon Sword* (Saddle Road Press), a cross-genre work of Zen koan and prose poems. A new book of prose poems, *The World Is God's Language*, will be published by Sixteen Rivers Press in 2021.

**Maxine Chernoff** — Since moving to the Bay Area in 1994, Maxine Chernoff has published three works of fiction and eight books of poems, most recently, *Under the Music: Selected Prose Poems*. She served as chair of Creative Writing at San Francisco State University for twenty years, where she remains a professor, and edited *New American Writing* with Paul Hoover. A winner of a 2013 NEA in poetry, she was a visiting writer at the American Academy in Rome in 2019. Her commute to work takes her over the Golden Gate Bridge from Mill Valley.

**Carolyn Chris** ("Lindy") was born and grew up in England but has spent most of her life in San Francisco. She ushers for the San Francisco Symphony and the San Francisco Opera House. She enjoys gardening, knitting, painting, history and writing. She lives with her small dog, Fiona, and her two cats — Parker and the ill-named Sweetie Pie. Her home is in the Crocker-Amazon, a quiet residential neighborhood near the Cow Palace. It's often omitted from City maps, but a few people have heard about the man who has a large cow on his roof, which he decorates weekly. Her neighbors speak English, Chinese, Italian, Tagalog and Spanish.

**Chris Cole** is a multi-media artist living in the Bay Area and also goes by the name, Disembodied Poetics. His novel, *Such Great Heights*, transplants *The Great Gatsby* to modern day Silicon Valley. He has a loyal internet following and publishes poetry and prose for both reputable and disreputable periodicals and anthologies. For the last decade he has helped run the San Francisco literary staple, Quiet Lightning.

**Lucille Lang Day** is the author of eleven poetry collections, most recently *Birds of San Pancho and Other Poems of Place* (Blue Light Press, 2020). She has also co-edited two anthologies, *Fire and Rain: Ecopoetry of California* and *Red Indian Road West: Native American Poetry from California*, and has published two children's books and a memoir, *Married at Fourteen*. Her honors include the Blue Light Poetry Prize, two Josephine Miles/PEN Oakland Literary Awards, the Joseph Henry Jackson Award, and eleven Pushcart Prize nominations. She earned her MFA in creative writing at San Francisco State University and never tired of driving across the bridge from Oakland to San Francisco.

**Joseph Di Prisco** was general manager of two restaurants in San Francisco, no longer in operation (long story, told in his memoir, *Subway to California*), and teacher for many years at University High School in San Francisco (a story also told in *Subway to California* and *The Pope of Brooklyn*). He lived in Berkeley forever, now out in the hinterlands of Contra Costa County. His new novel, *The Good Family Fitzgerald*, is a saga of money and Catholics, crime and angels — the Irish and the Italians. He is the founding chair of the Simpson Literary Project.

**Heather Saunders Estes** — After years as CEO of Planned Parenthood of Northern California, Heather Saunders Estes now writes poems about ravens, kale and glittering steps. Her first book, *Inner Sunset*, is named after her San Francisco neighborhood, where she can see a flash of ocean through trees to the west, Sutro Tower and Twin Peaks to the east. She has walked the city 13 years, adding to her map of the best vacant lots and corners of parks to pick ripe blackberries.

**Kathy Evans** is author of four books of poetry: *Trespassers Welcome, Imagination Comes To Breakfast, As The Heart is Held*, and *Hunger and Thirst*, winner of the Small Press Poetry Prize. She has taught with California Poets in the School at Marin County Juvenile Hall, at The University of San Francisco, at College of Marin, and the Osher Lifelong

Learning Institute. She was an artist-in-residence at the Headlands Center for the Arts, and is currently a poet-in-residence at The Benioff Children's Hospital in Oakland and San Francisco. She lives in San Rafael, California, by the library.

**Lawrence Ferlinghetti** is beloved in San Francisco. He served as first Poet Laureate of San Francisco, was the co-founder of City Lights Booksellers and Publishers, and was also a painter and social activist. He is the author of more than thirty books of poetry, including *Poetry as Insurgent Art*, *Americus, Book*; *A Far Rockaway of the Heart*; and *A Coney Island of the Mind*, his first collection of poems, which has been translated into nine languages and sold more than one million copies. He is the author of translations, fiction, theatre, art criticism, and film narration. Ferlinghetti turned 100 in 2019, leading the city of San Francisco to proclaim his birthday, March 24, "Lawrence Ferlinghetti Day."

**Elsa Fernandez** was born in India, but after 50 years in San Francisco, her cellular-memories tune to her big love for this city she calls home. After a corporate career, she retired in 2014 and rediscovered her love for the written word. She loves travel and once called in sick to overstay an Irish vacation by 8 weeks to play the piano at Sloopy's, a pub in Ranelagh. She writes for *Vistas & Byways*, the online journal for OLLI at San Francisco State University. You will often find her at Heron's Head Park in India Basin — a peaceful, restored salt marsh by the Bay, for waterfowl and shorebirds. "Listen for the loons," she advises.

**Stewart Florsheim** was born in New York City, the son of refugees from Hitler's Germany. He came to the Bay Area in 1976 to attend graduate school and never left! Stewart has been widely published in magazines and anthologies. He was the editor of *Ghosts of the Holocaust*, an anthology of poetry by children of Holocaust survivors (Wayne State University Press). His books include a chapbook, *The Girl Eating Oysters* (2River Press); and two full-length collections published by Blue Light Press — *The Short Fall From Grace*, winner of the 2005 Blue Light Book Award, and *A Split Second of Light*, which received Honors in the 2011 San Francisco Book Festival.

**Diane Frank** is author of eight books of poems, three novels, and a photo memoir of her 400 mile trek in the Himalayas. Her friends describe her as a harem of seven women in one very small body. She lives in the Outer Sunset in San Francisco, where she dances, plays cello, and creates her life as an art form. Diane teaches at San Francisco State University and Dominican University. She also plays cello in the Golden Gate Symphony. *Blackberries in the Dream House*, her first novel, won the Chelson Award for Fiction and was nominated for the Pulitzer Prize. Her new book, *While Listening to the Enigma Variations: New and Selected Poems* was published in 2021 by Glass Lyre Press.

**Elinor Gale** has been a writer and observer of human nature since childhood. An inveterate eavesdropper, she has woven her curiosity about human behavior into her work as a writing teacher, editor, and creator of humorous yet poignant fiction and poetry. Her debut novel, *The Emancipation of Emily Rosenbloom*, was published by Blue Light Press. A native New Englander, Elinor Gale came to California 20 years ago and is happily settled in San Francisco with her partner and his chubby Burmese cat.

**Joan Gelfand** — A lifelong resident of the San Francisco Bay Area, Joan Gelfand's reviews, stories, essays and poetry have appeared in over 150 national and international literary journals, including *The Huffington Post, Rattle, Levure Litterarie, Chicken Soup for the Soul*, and *The Meridien Anthology of Contemporary Poetry*. "The Ferlinghetti School of Poetics" was made into a short film by Dana Walden and has been shown at 20 international film festivals. *You Can Be a Winning Writer: The 4 C's of Author Success*, was a #1 bestseller on Amazon. Her debut novel, *Extreme*, was published by Blue Light Press in 2020. Joan lives in San Francisco with her husband, Adam Hertz, and two beatnik cats – Jack Kerouac and Lawrence Ferlinghetti.

**Joan Gerstein** — Just after I moved to Berkeley in 1969, I met a man who said he would be my tour guide in San Francisco. As driver, I followed his directions and found myself on the top of Lombard Street. Born and raised in flat Brooklyn and Long Island, I was so freaked out having to traverse the steep hairpin turns. Fifty years later, I am still not comfortable driving those hills, especially when I am stopped going uphill at a red light.

**Kathryn Santana Goldman** is a San Francisco native who grew up in the Bayview District. Diversity was never something to call out because everyone came from a different background. The City was filled with an amazing mix of colorful characters: Emperor Norton, the North Beach Twins, Carol Doda, Mayor Sutro, and Alma Spreckles. Even some notorious folks made their mark. *"My dad died five years ago, and while cleaning out his dresser, I found a picture of him standing next to Hoffa!"* Kathryn enjoys writing poetry and using photography to archive her changing landscape.

**Vince Gotera** was born and raised in San Francisco. He grew up in the Haight-Ashbury and was a teenager during the advent of the hippies and the Summer of Love. "As a lead guitarist," Vince says, "I was influenced by the rock bands that played around The City: Jefferson Airplane, Big Brother and the Holding Company, The Charlatans, The Grateful Dead, Quicksilver, Santana, and many others. In fact, I fondly remember being an eighth grader at St. Agnes School on Ashbury and hearing The Dead rehearsing in their house across the street." Vince left in 1982 for grad school in the Midwest and has not lived in The City since then. "But I am always excited to visit and enjoy the dazzling diversity, charming neighborhoods, and utter beauty of San Francisco, forever home."

**Ken Haas** has been published in more than fifty journals, including *Cottonwood, Existere, The Helix, Natural Bridge, Quiddity*, and *Spoon River*. He won the Betsy Colquitt Poetry Award and serves on the Board of Directors of the Community of Writers. He received an MA in English from the University of Sussex, U.K., where he wrote his dissertation on Wallace Stevens. The son of European immigrants, Ken grew up in New York City but has lived for the past 44 years in San Francisco, where he sponsors a weekly poetry writing program at UCSF Children's Hospital.

**Katharine Harer**'s poetry has been published in seven small press editions. Her new collection, *Deconfliction*, came out in 2020 from fmsbw press in San Francisco, and her new and selected poems, *Jazz & Other Hot Subjects*, was published by Bombshelter Press. Nonfiction projects include interviews with women who played pro baseball and a travel memoir about Pablo Neruda. Katharine teaches English at Skyline

Community College, where she is Vice President for the teachers' union. She teaches creative writing at the San Francisco Writing Salon and lives in San Rafael with her husband, Bob, and their dog, Ozzie. She grew up in San Francisco, where her father worked as a longshoreman and her mother worked as a bookkeeper for the Elevator Constructors Union at 22nd and Mission.

**Katherine Hastings**, author of three collections of poetry, grew up in the Cow Hollow neighborhood of San Francisco before it was flooded with tourism and technology. When the cost of living rose, she moved to Sonoma County where she served as Poet Laureate from 2014 - 2016 and hosted a poetry-focused radio program on NPR affiliate KRCB. She volunteered on Alcatraz Island as a researcher and writer and made regular visits to her childhood backyards of the Palace of Fine Arts and San Francisco Bay. Following the 2017 wildfires in Sonoma County, she moved to an island between Buffalo and Canada. She is surrounded by water. Her poems will always be rooted in San Francisco.

**Jack Hirschman** is an emeritus Poet Laureate of San Francisco (2006-2009), a founding member of the Revolutionary Poets Brigade of San Francisco and of the World Poetry Movement of Medellin, Colombia. His masterwork are 3 thousand-page books of poems called *The Arcanes*, published in the American Language in Salerno, Italy. He is a cultural worker for the League of Revolutionaries for a New America (LRNA).

**Jodi Hottel** is a *sansei*, third generation Japanese American. She is author of three chapbooks: *Out of the Ashes* (Pandemonium Press), *Voyeur* (WordTech Press), and *Heart Mountain* (Blue Light Press). *Heart Mountain*, her chapbook of poems about the Japanese American incarceration, was winner of the 2012 Blue Light Press Poetry Prize. San Francisco was an area with a large Japanese American population at the time of the incarceration. Most of those families were initially taken to a temporary detention site at the Tanforan race track in San Bruno, now the site of a shopping mall.

**Erik Ievins** — Music has always been a comfortable second language for Erik Ievins. Classically trained on cello since he was old enough to hold a bow, Erik joined professional symphony and pops orchestras while still in high school. He plays for contra dances, Scottish dances and English Country dances with StringFire, and volunteers in the cello section of the Golden Gate Symphony. When collaborating with poets, he expresses the emotions of the poem through music. From time to time, when he's not tinkering with cars or rebuilding houses, he is moved to document his surroundings with the written word.

**Elise Kazanjian** claims that rare right to say she is a native San Franciscan born in this beautiful city. After living in other countries, she still thinks this city is unmatched for its beauty and diversity. She has been a San Francisco pawnbroker; has been published in various anthologies and journals, including *Poets Eleven* and *New Millenium*; has worked as Foreign Editor, CCTV, Beijing, China. She is currently co-judge of the Prose Poem Category, Soul-Making Keats Literary Competition.

**Stephen Kessler** is a long-time resident of Northern California and is frequently found in San Francisco. His recent books of poems are *Garage Elegies* and *Last Call* (Black Widow Press). His translation of *Save Twilight: Selected Poems* by Julio Cortazar (City Lights) received the 2017 Northern California Book Award for Poetry in Translation. His versions of Luis Cernuda have received a Lambda Literary Award, the PEN Center USA Translation Award, and the Harold Morton Landon Translation Award from the Academy of American Poets. He writes a weekly op-ed column in the *Santa Cruz Sentinel*.

**Phyllis Klein** has a psychotherapy office in the Flood Building in San Francisco. She's been working in the city for over 35 years, having moved to SF from Michigan in 1984. Her office has been empty since mid-March while she works online from home during the pandemic. During this time, her first book of poetry, *The Full Moon Herald*, was published.

**Jennifer Lagier** lives near the Pacific Ocean with two spoiled rescue dogs. A regular participant in Blue Light Press online workshops and writing retreats, she taught with California Poets in the Schools, worked as an educator, and married a man from the Sunset District in San Francisco. Blue Light Press published her book, *Harbingers*, in 2016 and *Meditations on Seascapes and Cypress*, in 2021.

**Daniel J. Langton** taught English Literature and Creative Writing at San Francisco State University for 50 years. His work has appeared in *Poetry*, the *Paris Review*, *The Nation*, *Atlantic Monthly*, *Iowa Review*, *Vallum* and *Fiddlehead*. His latest collection is *Personal Effects* (Blue Light Press, 2014).

**Ibu Robin Lim** is a Filipina-American-Micronesian midwife and founder of Bumi Sehat in Indonesia, a non-profit which builds and maintains medical relief and childbirth clinics in Bali, Aceh, Lombok and Papua, Indonesia, and the Philippines. Ibu (Mother) Robin also travels the world to provide disaster relief after tsunamis, earthquakes, volcanic eruptions, typhoons, and other calamities fueled by the Climate Crisis. In 2011 Ibu Robin was chosen CNN Hero of the Year. Her books include *After the Baby's Birth, Wellness for Mothers, Ecology of Gentle Birth, Awakening Birth, Eating for Two, Placenta the Forgotten Chakra, Eat Pray Doula, The Geometry of Splitting Souls* (poetry), *Butterfly People* (a novel), and *The Natural Family Planning Workbook*. As a child, Lim often stayed in San Francisco with her aunties, Josephine and Lourdes Lim, who survived the infamous Bataan Death March and immigrated to America after World War II. Her passion is respectful, gentle childbirth, and healthcare as a human right.

**Ellaraine Lockie** lives in the South Bay but also feels at home in San Francisco. She thinks of our area as one big sea of buildings with San Francisco as the anchor. For forty-plus years it has been the cultural ballast for the writer, artist and musician that live inside her. She's thankful, too, for the many houseguests whom she suspects have been lured to visit because of "The City" as much or more than her.

**Alison Luterman** has published four books of poems, including *Desire Zoo* (Tia Chucha Press) and *In the Time of Great Fires*, winner of the Catamaran Poetry Prize. Her work has been published in *The Sun*, *Rattle*, *Nimrod*, and many other journals and anthologies. She also writes personal essays, plays, and musicals. She teaches memoir and poetry through The Writing Salon in Berkeley. "Fog" was originally published in rattle.com. She wrote the first version of "Making My Way Down Market Street" on BART. "I live in Oakland, but came into SF to see a play on Market Street. Making my way back to BART, I was struck by the scenes of devastation I was walking past. I began writing this poem in the BART station waiting for my train, and continued it as we rattled through the tunnel and back to the East Bay."

**Robin Lysne** — I love saying to my Midwestern friends: "Only in San Francisco!" Most of my adult life, I have lived in the San Francisco Bay Area as an author of seven books, an artist, and Energy Medicine Practitioner. Only in San Francisco could I be all that I am without anyone raising their hands in horror. My books range from creating personal rituals (*Ceremonies from the Heart*) to Energy Medicine (*Heart Path, Heart Path Handbook*) and two poetry books, (*Mosaic* and *Poems for the Lost Deer*) all published by Blue Bone Books. It is a delight to be included in *Fog and Light*.

**Diane K. Martin** moved to San Francisco in 1976. She has lived on 10th, 20th, and 30th Avenues, in the Richmond District, and later on Ashton Avenue in the Ingleside. Her poems have appeared in *American Poetry Review, Field, Kenyon Review, Tin House, ZYZZYVA*, and many other journals. She has two books of poems: *Conjugated Visits* and *Hue & Cry*.

**Kathleen McClung** fell in love with San Francisco at age nine when she came with her mother on a Greyhound bus to see "Carmen" at the War Memorial Opera House. She cried when they had to leave at the intermission to catch the bus back to Sacramento. Kathleen has had the great good fortune to live, teach, and write on the foggy west side of San Francisco for over thirty years. Her books include *Three Soul-Makers, A Juror Must Fold in on Herself, Temporary Kin, The Typists Play Monopoly,* and *Almost the Rowboat*.

**Susie Meserve** moved to the Inner Richmond District in the summer of 2005, where she wore a wool sweater every day. After writing a series of poems inspired by the fog, the Russian church, the dim sum shops on Clement Street, and the many wonders of Golden Gate Park, she and her husband moved to the Castro, where it was marginally less foggy. After three years in San Francisco, they moved to Norway for a year, then to the East Bay. Susie is the author of *Little Prayers*, which won the 2018 Blue Light Book Award. She also has a chapbook, *Faith*. She teaches writing in San Francisco.

**Carolyn Miller** lives in a Romeo and Juliet flat on the Hyde Street cable-car line in San Francisco, where she writes, paints, and works as a freelance writer and editor. Her books of poetry are *Route 66 and Its Sorrows* (Terrapin Books), *After Cocteau* and *Light, Moving,* both from Sixteen Rivers Press. She moved to San Francisco in 1970 and loves it just as much, if not more, than she did then.

**Angie Minkin** has lived in San Francisco for 40 years and is grateful to live under a sky filled with sea light. She raised two children in San Francisco's Excelsior District and now shares her home with her husband and two playful cats. Angie is inspired by the political landscape, the poetry of liberation, and the voice of the wise woman. She is proud to be a co-author of *Dreams and Blessings, Six Visionary Poets,* recently published by Blue Light Press. A poetry editor of *Vistas & Byways,* Angie's work has appeared in that journal and several others.

**Matthew M. Monte** was born across the bridge in Marin County, which he had the good sense to flee in his teens. He lived on the island of O'ahu for many years and studied Botany at the University of Hawaii-Manoa when he wasn't surfing or playing slack key guitar with his friends. His debut book of poems, *The Case of the Six-Sided Dream,* won the 2017 Blue Light Poetry Prize. Words attached to his name have appeared in *Sidestream, Creosote Journal, Transfer, The Racket, Ashcan Magazine,* and the *Poets 11* Anthologies (2014 and 2016). He lives in San Francisco with his wife and son, across the street from the Pacific Ocean, where 97% of his ideas ride ashore and take shape in the world's finest city.

**Alejandro Murguía** is the author of *This War Called Love, Nine Stories* (City Lights Books) winner of the American Book Award. He is a founding member and the first director of The Mission Cultural Center for Latino Arts. Currently, he is a professor in Latina/Latino Studies at San Francisco State University. In 2013 City Lights Books published his book, *Stray Poems.* His short story "The Other Barrio" was recently released as a full length feature, filmed in the streets of the Mission District. He was the Sixth San Francisco Poet Laureate and the first Latino to hold the position.

**Marsha M. Nelson** was born in Trinidad and lives on Long Island, New York. She visited San Francisco in August of 2018 to attend the Blue Light Press Summer Writing Workshop and fell in love with San Francisco. She is a playwright, screenwriter, and award-winning poet. Her poem, "I Thought It Was Love," won the Nassau County Poet Laureate Society 2016 award. Her chapbook, *Night Visions,* was published by Blue Light Press.

**Gail Newman**'s poems have appeared in journals including *Nimrod International Journal, Prairie Schooner* and *Spillway* and in anthologies including *The Doll Collection, Ghosts of the Holocaust, Healing the Divide: Poems of Kindness and Connection (forthcoming) and America, We Call Your Name.* Her book of poetry, *One World,* was published by Moon Tide Press. Her new collection, *Blood Memory,* published in 2020, was chosen by Marge Piercy for the Marsh Hawk Press Poetry Award.

**Gwynn O'Gara** grew up in San Francisco and left many times, almost always coming back. For 25 years she worked as a California Poet in the Schools and served as Sonoma County Poet Laureate 2010-2011. She enjoys reciting poems of the ecstatic tradition with Rumi's Caravan. Her books include *Snake Woman Poems* and the chapbooks *Fixer-Upper, Winter at Green Haven, Fruit of Life,* and *Sea Cradles.*

**Meg Pokrass** is the author of six fiction collections, two novellas-in-flash and a collection of prose poetry. She is the recipient of the Blue Light Book Award for *Cellulose Pajamas* (2016) and *Spinning to Mars* (2021). Her microfictions have appeared in hundreds of journals, most recently, *Washington Square Review and Electric Literature.* She recently moved from San Francisco to a tiny market town in England near the Scottish border.

**Karen Poppy** has work published in *The Cortland Review* (Best of the Net nomination), *Naugatuck River Review* (Contest Finalist for the poem "Marina Safeway, San Francisco"), *The Gay and Lesbian Review Worldwide, ArLiJo,* and *Wallace Stevens Journal.* Her chapbook, *Crack Open/Emergency,* is published by Finishing Line Press, with two new chapbooks forthcoming. An attorney licensed in California and Texas, she lives in the San Francisco Bay Area.

**Barbara Quick** — Novelist and poet Barbara Quick was co-winner of the 2020 Blue Light Press Poetry Prize for her chapbook, *The Light on Sifnos*. Her fourth novel, *What Disappears*, is being brought out by Regal House in 2022. *Vivaldi's Virgins*, her second novel — which has been translated into a dozen languages — provided the rationale, a decade ago, for a blind date with a violist of the San Francisco Symphony. They've been married for nearly ten years, and she is now immersed in the world of classical music and musicians. She believes she would win the prize, if one were given, for the orchestra spouse who attends concerts most regularly and devotedly at Davies Symphony Hall.

**Jane Rades** grew up in Wisconsin, then moved out to San Francisco in 1963 to attend the San Francisco Art Institute. She has been in San Francisco ever since except for a year in the high desert of New Mexico. She moved back to San Francisco because she missed the fog, the cable cars, and the other poets. Jane has published two books of poetry, *Five Decades, A Rosary of Poems* and *Midnight at Mom and Dad's*. She also published a book on the Tarot, *Two Years in the Tarot, Portrait of the Artist as a Young Fortuneteller*, along with a deck of Tarot cards, *The 1969 Tarot*.

**Alice Elizabeth Rogoff** — "The first street I lived on in San Francisco was in North Beach. I would walk to the original Intersection and hear poets. From meeting people at a bookstore reading, I was published in *The San Francisco Bark: An Anthology of Bay Area Poets*. I now live in the Sunnyside District near City College. I have been a part of several writers groups including Noe Valley Poets, the *Haight Ashbury Literary Journal*, and the LaborFest Writers Group. My most recent poetry book, *Painting the Cat's Vision*, was published by Blue Light Press."

**Robert Scotellaro** worked at the U.S. Mint in San Francisco for many years and currently lives in the Excelsior District of the City. He is the author of seven literary chapbooks and five full-length collections of flash and micro fiction, including *Measuring the Distance, What We Know So far, Bad Motel*, and *Nothing Is Ever One Thing*, and *What Are the Chances?* (Press 53). Robert is co-editor of *New Micro: Exceptionally Short Fiction*, published by W. W. Norton & Company. He is one of the founding donors to the Ransom Flash Fiction Collection at the University of Texas, Austin.

**Amy Smith** is a geographer and researcher studying transportation and cities. Born and raised in Florida, Amy moved to California in 2009 and has been a San Francisco resident since 2013. Her poetry has previously appeared in the *Haight Ashbury Literary Journal*, *Cathexis Northwest Press*, and *Sparkle & Blink*.

**Jeanine Stevens** — In San Francisco for many meetings and visits, Jeanine thought she was pretty good at directions, planned the route ahead of time, maps on the seat beside her. She would invariably take a wrong turn and in no time end up at the ocean. After a few detours like this, she laughed at her self-confidence and realized that if she slowed down and followed light, she always ended up at water's edge. Jeanine studied poetry at U.C. Davis, has an M.A. in Anthropology and an Ed.D in Education. She is author of three books and several chapbooks. Jeanine found her special tree for "forest bathing" right in her own back yard, a sprawling laurel with multiple trunks. She also enjoys collage and Romanian folk dancing.

**Michael Angelo Tata** relocated from Miami to San Francisco for a JD fellowship at Golden Gate University School of Law. Most recently, he guest edited the digital collection *Convoluting the Dialectical Image* for Taylor & Francis. It examines the work of German philosopher Walter Benjamin through a kaleidoscope of interdisciplinary approaches. His poem for this book consists of 9 haikus originally posted to his social media between 2018 and 2020. He lives in Lower Nob Hill, and his chapbook, *The Multiplication of Joy into Integers*, won the Blue Light Poetry Prize.

**Susan Terris** — "I grew up in St. Louis, went to college on the East Coast, but all of my adult life has been in San Francisco. I've lived more than 50 years now in a house near the Presidio that is about a mile from the AT&T Baseball Stadium and another mile from Ocean Beach. The Presidio has always been my urban forest. I know all its streets and alleys and all of its trails. Once when I was starting out on a trail, I found a rusting Schwinn bicycle in the high weeds next to some blackberry bushes. As I walked on, I was thinking how much more I liked being alone in the woods than pedaling a man-made metal bike amid honking cars on an asphalt street. Recent books are *Familiar Tense*;

*Take Two: Film Studies; Memos;* and *Ghost of Yesterday: New & Selected Poems.* "Abandoned Bicycle" was first published in *Poetry Flash* in 2012.

**Jane Underwood** — As the founder of *The Writing Salon*, a unique creative writing school in San Francisco and Berkeley that she directed for 16 years, Jane Underwood was a beloved mentor. Her poetry, essays and erotica appeared in *The San Francisco Chronicle, Salon, The Sun Magazine, Yellow Silk,* and *Best Women's Erotica,* and she was also a gifted photographer. After being diagnosed with cancer in 2005, she kept an online blog at "My Great Breast Cancer Adventure" and returned to her early love of poetry with renewed purpose. Her book, *When My Heart Goes Dark, I Turn the Porch Light On,* was published by Blue Light Press in 2017.

**Hollace Anne Veldhuis** was born in Manhattan in 1946 and grew up in suburban New Jersey. She studied English literature and poetics at Oberlin and SUNY Buffalo. In 1970, like many others, she moved to San Francisco, bringing her many notebooks with her. She settled in Bernal Heights, where she still enjoys the narrow streets, the gorgeous views and several generations of eccentric, creative people. In retirement she has found renewed energy and time for writing. Her poems have been published in *Intro 2, The Sky Away from Here,* and *The Avocet.*

**Will Walker** has lived in San Francisco since 1973. He was an editor of the *Haight Ashbury Literary Journal* for seven years and has two books of poetry, *Wednesday after Lunch* and *Zeus at Twilight,* published by Blue Light Press. His poetry has appeared in *Across Borders, Alabama Literary Reiew, Burningword, The Chiron Review, Passager, Street Sheet,* and many other journals. He lives in the Haight with his wife, Valerie, and their dog. He shares, "You know what they say: In the East, nothing works and everything matters. In the West, everything works, and nothing matters. All in all, I prefer the West."

**George Wallace** is writer in residence at the Walt Whitman Birthplace, first Poet Laureate of the National Beat Festival, and winner of numerous international prizes, including the Alexander Medal and the Orpheus Prize. He is a New York native who has lived in many parts of the world, including San Francisco's Mission District. His book

*Smashing Rock And Straight As Razors* was a book award winner with San Francisco's Blue Light Press. His new book, *Resistance is a Blue Spanish Guitar,* is forthcoming from Blue Light Press.

**Mary Winegarden** — In early 1974, she hitchhiked with her Brit partner, Geoff Hoyle, to San Francisco from a commune in the Ozark Mountains. They were a part of the Pickle Family Circus, finally settling in Noe Valley, where they raised their three children. She taught English and Comparative Literature at San Francisco State for many years. Her first poetry collection, *The Translator's Sister,* won an American Book Award in 2012. Recent poems have appeared in the *Squaw Valley Review, Rosebud, Catamaran, West Marin Review* and *parentheses.* A swimmer, grandmother and poet-activist, she has moved north to Point Reyes, but will always think of San Francisco as home.

# Permissions and Acknowledgements

"Dog" by Lawrence Ferlinghetti, from *A Coney Island of the Mind,* © 1958 by Lawrence Ferlinghetti. Reprinted by permission of New Directions Publishing Corporation. Note: "a seriously dog" was corrected to "a serious dog" on 10/20/2010.

Abby Caplin: "Bird and Beckett Bookstore San Francisco" was previously published in *Willow Review*. "Dog Path at Fort Funston, San Francisco" was published previously in *Forge*, July 2015.

Dane Cervine: "Earth Is A Fickle Dancer" first appeared in *Catamaran*; "Something to Live For" first appeared in the *Iconoclast*; both poems appear in the book *Earth Is A Fickle Dancer* (Main Street Rag).

Lucille Lang Day: "710 Ashbury, 1967" was published in *The Curvature of Blue* and first published in *Re)verb*. "András Schiff Plays Bach's English Suites" was first published in *California Quarterly*.

Joseph Di Prisco: "The Bar at the End of Some Other Road" first appeared *in Sightlines from the Cheap Seats.*

Heather Saunders Estes: "Sing-Along Messiah" and "Tree #143" were first published in her first book of poems, *Inner Sunset* (Blue Light Press, 2019).

Diane Frank: All poems in this book are published in *While Listening to the Enigma Variations: New and Selected Poems* (Glass Lyre Press). "Earthquake, 5 A.M." and "Ultra-Body Over the Mountain" are also published in *Canon for Bears and Ponderosa Pines* (Glass Lyre Press).

Joan Gelfand: "The Ferlinghetti School of Poetics," was made into a short film by Dana Walden and has been shown at 20 international film festivals.

Vince Gotera: "Childhood," "Free Ride," "The Front Door," and "Doggie Diner, Geary and Arguello, 1969" all appeared in Silver Birch Press.

Ken Haas: All poems published in *Fog and Light* were previously published in *Borrowed Light* (Red Mountain Press).

Katharine Harer: "Why I Like Graffiti" and "Love Note to San Francisco" first appeared in her book, *Jazz & Other Hot Subjects* (bombshelter press).

Katherine Hastings: "Clouds" first appeared in *Cloud Fire — Poems*, by Katherine Hastings. "The Dawn is a Mirror of Myself" was published in *Nighthawks — Poems*, by Katherine Hastings.

Diane K. Martin: "Contiguous" was previously published in the *Crab Orchard Review, The West Coast and Beyond* anthology.

Ellaraine Lockie: "Edge of Night" was first published by *Taproot Literary Review*.

Kathleen McClung: "Renter Sonnet #3" was previously published in *The Typists Play Monopoly* and first appeared in *Mezzo Cammin*. "Why We Have Windows" was previously published in *Almost the Rowboat* and first appeared in *Poets 11 2010: An Anthology of Poems*.

Susie Meserve: "Fog" was first published in *Little Prayers* (Blue Light Press, 2018).

Carolyn Miller: "Things to Be Grateful for in San Francisco" was first published in *World Made of Desire* (Protean Press). "Riding the 30 Stockton" was first published in *After Cocteau* (Sixteen Rivers Press). "Sunset on the 38 Geary" was first published in *Route 66 and Its Sorrows*, (Terrapin Books).

Angie Minkin: "Ode to Lucca Ravioli" was first published (in slightly different form) in the Fall 2019 issue of *Vistas & Byways*.

Gail Newman: "Where I Live" was previously published in *The Other Side of the Postcard* (City Lights Foundation Books).

Alice Elizabeth Rogoff: "Mission Street Station" was previously published in *PoetryMagazine.com* and in *Barge Wood* (C.C. Marimbo).

Robert Scotellaro: "Bookends" was originally published in *Measuring the Distance*. "Measuring the Distance" was originally published in *Gargoyle*. "After the Earthquake" was originally published in *Willows Wept Review*.

Amy Smith: "Ode to the L Owl" was first published in the *Haight Ashbury Literary Journal*.

Jane Underwood: All poems published in Fog and Light were previously published in *When My Heart Goes Dark, I Turn the Porch Light On* (Blue Light Press, 2017).

CPSIA information can be obtained
at www.ICGtesting.com
Printed in the USA
FSHW011949310321
80053FS